The Family Tree Guide To
Finding Your Ellis Island Ancestors

The Family Tree

Guide To Finding Your
ELLIS ISLAND
ANCESTORS

SHARON DeBARTOLO CARMACK

FAMILY TREE BOOKS
CINCINNATI, OHIO
www.familytreemagazine.com

Other fine Family Tree Books are available from your local bookstore or on our Web site at www.familytreemagazine.com.

09 08 07 06 05   5 4 3 2 1

Library of Congress Cataloging-in-Publication Data

Carmmack, Sharon DeBartolo
   The family tree guide to finding your Ellis Island ancestors : a genealogist's essential guide to navigating the Ellis Island database and passenger arrival list / by Sharon DeBartolo Carmack.
      p.   cm.
   Includes bibliographical references and index.
   ISBN 1-55870-694-1
   1. United States—Genealogy—Handbooks, manuals, etc. 2. United States—Emigration and immigration—Handbooks, manuals, etc. 3. Ellis Island Immigration Station (N.Y. and N.J.)—Registers—Handbooks, manuals, etc. I. Title.
   CS49.C383   2005
   929'.1'07207471—dc22   2005000115
                                                                CIP

Editor: Erin Nevius
Production coordinator: Robin Richie
Assistant production coordinator: Logan Cummins
Interior designer: Sandy Conopeotis Kent
Cover design by Stephanie Goodrich
Icon designer: Cindy Beckmeyer

DEDICATION

What would a book on Ellis Island be without a dedication to my forebears who processed there, giving me a reason to become obsessed with the subject? So this book is dedicated to my great-grandparents Salvatore and Angelina (Vallarelli) Ebetino and their children, and Albino and Lucia (Vallarelli) DeBartolo and their children, as well as their siblings and cousins who made the journey from Terlizzi, Bari, Italy, in the early twentieth century.

This book is also dedicated to my great-great-grandmother, Isabella (Veneto) Vallarelli. Although she came through the Port of Boston, this four-foot-tall woman came alone in 1916 at the age of 63 so she could be closer to her children and grandchildren. It took more courage than I would have had.

About the Author

Sharon DeBartolo Carmack is a Certified Genealogist specializing in writing and editing family history narratives. She has authored fifteen books and hundreds of articles and columns that have appeared in nearly every major genealogical journal and publication. As executive editor of Family Tree Books (formerly Betterway Books), she has acquired and edited more than thirty-five titles, making Family Tree Books and Betterway Books America's best-selling guides to genealogy.

Sharon is a partner in Warren, Carmack & Associates, a genealogical research and consulting firm specializing in Irish, Italian, American Indian, and onsite research at the National Archives, the Family History Library, and in Ireland.

Since 1998, Sharon has served on the Statue of Liberty-Ellis Island Foundation's History Advisory Committee. Her awards and honors include APG's Grahame Thomas Smallwood Jr. Award of Merit (1990); the Federation of Genealogical Societies' Award of Merit (1992 and 2002); and in 1998, Sharon was made a Fellow of the Utah Genealogical Association for her "outstanding contributions to the genealogical community and for the production of articles, books, and lectures that are an exemplary blend of her expertise in history and genealogy."

Sharon can be reached through her Web site: <www.SharonCarmack.com>.

Acknowledgments

My interest in Ellis Island began nearly two decades ago, when I discovered that my Italian grandparents were processed there in the early twentieth century. Once I learned this, I wanted to know what the experience was like for them. At the time, my remaining living immigrant relatives had come through Ellis Island when they were small children, and they only remembered bits and pieces. I had to fill in the holes with other sources.

In the early 1980s when my interest was sparked, the Island had just begun renovations on the main building. My father was working for the Department of the Interior and had friends in the National Parks Service. Through his connections, I was able to walk the echoing halls before workmen descended upon the Island, making it into one of New York's largest museums.

Since its renovation, I've been on the Island many times, as a tourist and as part of the History Advisory Committee for the Statue of Liberty-Ellis Island Foundation's American Family Immigration History Center. In serving on that committee, I was fortunate to meet and work with the nation's leading immigration historians. My journey to learn everything I could about the Ellis Island experience came from reading many of their works on the subject, and in talking and corresponding with the historians and librarians at Ellis Island, including Barry Moreno and Jeffrey S. Dosik. They were all valuable sources, as were Daniel Lynch and Peg Zitko, who provided me with advance information about revisions to the Ellis Island Web site.

Marian L. Smith of the U.S. Citizenship and Immigration Services (formerly the Immigration and Naturalization Service) has always been patient and helpful in answering questions relating to passenger arrival lists and other immigration records. She graciously granted permission for me to reprint her compelling article on the retention and destruction of the Ellis Island passenger lists in Appendix A.

Throughout the years, three genealogists have clipped and sent me articles on Ellis Island or assisted me in obtaining records: Anita A. Lustenberger, Roger D. Joslyn, and Suzanne McVetty. This "New York Trio" has always been generous with their time, eagerly opened their homes to me when I visited New York, and took me by the hand when I rode the subways.

Erin Nevius, my colleague in publishing and associate editor at Family Tree Books, gave valuable suggestions to draft chapters and was the editor for this book. She works hard behind the scenes to make our books shine, and she deserves more credit than she's ever given.

To Clare (Rowan) Warren and Becky Shy for making their opinions—and their presence—known, whether I'm at home or in Ireland.

And finally, to James W. Warren, three roses in return. No one was more surprised than I.

Critical Acclaim for Author
Sharon DeBartolo Carmack

You Can Write Your Family History

"Step by step Sharon Carmack shows how to turn names and dates into real human beings for a family history. Anyone who has ever had thoughts about writing a family history will want to have this book to refer to again and again."
  —Henry B. Hoff, CG, FASG
    Editor, *The New England Historical and Genealogical Register*

"Engaging and informative, *You Can Write a Family History* shows family historians how to 'add life and history' to the genealogical facts they've gathered. Carmack shares the elements of the writer's craft—plot, character, and description—and illustrates how they can be used in preparing a family history for publication."
  —Ann Hege Huges
    President, Gateway Press, Inc.

"Almost all genealogists want to share the fruits of their research with the rest of the family, but fear that their relatives won't be interested in a standard genealogy. Sharon Carmack shows us how to create a family history that is much more than basic genealogy, a book that will be read and enjoyed for generations to come."
  —Harry Macy, FASG
    Editor, *The New York Genealogical and Biographical Record*

Your Guide to Cemetery Research

" . . . the most comprehensive book to date helping genealogists get the most out of cemeteries . . .at the same time celebrating their art, history, and beauty. Well worth the buy."
  —Steve Johnson, Interment.net

"Highly informative, covering a number of areas in great detail, and offering information otherwise not found in genealogy resources today."
  —William Spurlock, SavingGraves.com

"Genealogists and local historians of all stripes will find this book invaluable. Highly recommended for public and genealogy libraries."
  —*Library Journal*

"This new book maintains [Carmack's] high standard . . . . This is easily the most comprehensive guide I have seen on the subject."
  —*Louisiana Genealogical Register*

Organizing Your Family History Search
A Book of the Month Club Selection

"This book will provide comfort to those who shudder at the mounds of paper involved in a genealogical search. Carmack's solutions are inventive and flexible enough to fit any researcher. This very useful source is highly recommended."
　　—*Library Journal*

"Sharon DeBartolo Carmack's newest book . . . is the answer to a researcher's prayers. Everyone can benefit from the organizational tips offered by professionals that are interspersed throughout the book. As delightful to read as it is helpful . . . ."
　　—*Branches & Twigs*

A Genealogist's Guide to Discovering
Your Immigrant and Ethnic Ancestors

"Sharon Carmack has another title to her credit . . . . Over half the book is an excellent general genealogical guide . . . . The net result is a very useful guide for any American genealogist."
　　—*The New York Genealogical and Biographical Record*

"Ms. Carmack succeeds in her aim to help the heritage searcher identify and trace immigrant ancestors back to their arrival in America . . . . The book merits high marks for its scope and the variety of suggested data sources. Its easy-to-understand directions for pursuing them convey an atmosphere of enjoyable experience."
　　—*Pennsylvania Genealogical Magazine*

"Carmack's suggestions for learning more about one's own family through foods, customs, heirlooms, and stories are as valuable as her tips for conducting oral history interviews and handling family 'myths.' "
　　—Federation of Genealogical Societies' *Forum*

A Genealogist's Guide to Discovering Your Female Ancestors

"At last! This is the first guide to focus on the special strategies needed to track down your elusive female ancestors. Sharon DeBartolo Carmack has written an outstanding book. It is required reading!"
　　—*New England Historic Genealogical Society*

"Until now, no guide was devoted solely to finding information about women. This important book fills that void."
　　— *National Genealogical Society Quarterly*

Other Books by Sharon DeBartolo Carmack

GENEALOGICAL GUIDEBOOKS

You Can Write Your Family History
Your Guide to Cemetery Research
A Genealogist's Guide to Discovering Your Immigrant and Ethnic Ancestors
Organizing Your Family History Search
A Genealogist's Guide to Discovering Your Female Ancestors
The Genealogy Sourcebook
Italian-American Family History: A Guide to Researching and Writing About Your Heritage

FAMILY HISTORY NARRATIVES/COMPILED GENEALOGIES

Italians in Transition: The Vallarelli Family of Terlizzi, Italy, and Westchester County, New York and The DeBartolo Family of Terlizzi, Italy, New York, and San Francisco, California
A Sense of Duty: The Life and Times of Jay Roscoe Rhoads and his wife, Mary Grace Rudolph
My Wild Irish Rose: The Life of Rose (Norris) (O'Connor) Fitzhugh and her mother Delia (Gordon) Norris
David and Charlotte Hawes (Buckner) Stuart of King George County, Virginia, Including Three Generations of Their Descendants
American Lives and Lines, co-authored with Roger D. Joslyn
The Ebetino and Vallarelli Family History: Italian Immigrants to Westchester County, New York

PUBLISHED ABSTRACTS

Communities at Rest: An Inventory and Field Study of Five Eastern Colorado Cemeteries

Table of Contents At a Glance

Table of Contents

Foreword

By Stephen A. Briganti, President and CEO of The Statue of Liberty-Ellis Island Foundation

T he story of immigration is the story of America. From before our country's founding right up to the present day, we have been and remain a nation of immigrants. The hopes and dreams of freedom, opportunity, and a new life that beckoned to millions over the last four centuries are the same hopes and dreams that burn in the hearts of those coming to our shores today.

Nowhere was this saga more dramatically played out than at Ellis Island. This small spit of land in New York Harbor, in the shadow of the Statue of Liberty, witnessed the largest human migration in modern history. Ellis Island opened as the first United States federal immigration processing center on January 1, 1892, and during its peak years of operation through 1924, over 17 million new arrivals were processed. Most traveled in steerage—the bottom of the boat—and had to pass both physical and mental inspection before they were allowed through the "Golden Door" to their new life. It is this dramatic story—the Peopling of America®—which unfolds at the Ellis Island Immigration Museum.

The Statue of Liberty-Ellis Island Foundation was instituted in 1982 to raise the funds for and oversee the restorations of these two great monuments to freedom, working in partnership with the U.S. Department of the Interior/ National Parks Service. After restoring the Statue of Liberty for her glorious centennial in 1986, we turned our attention in earnest to restoring the Main Registry Building on Ellis Island—which was the largest historic restoration in U.S. history—and creating a world-class museum to explore, elucidate, and celebrate the immigrant experience.

But we learned something when those museum doors opened in September 1990. Visitors came in huge numbers—over 25 million to date—not only to view the museum's films and exhibits, but also to research the Ellis Island immigration records. But there was a problem: The immigration records weren't there! They were still only available on microfilm at the National Archives and Records Administration. While it was the Foundation's dream, even in the 1980s, to make those records accessible at Ellis Island, financial and technology constraints had made that impossible. But by the mid-1990s, that was going to change.

In 1995, the Foundation and the National Park Service entered into a partnership with The Church of Jesus Christ of Latter-day Saints to make this dream a reality. An army of twelve thousand LDS volunteers worked an amazing 5.6 million hours to create a database by extracting from the original microfilm the immigration data on the 25 million individuals who entered the Port of New York between 1892–1924. The Foundation then designed an exciting, interactive research facility—the American Family Immigration History Center®—to make these records available to the Ellis Island Museum visitors. In addition, <www.ellisisland.org> was created so people across the country and around the globe could access these records as well. When the Center and Web site launched on April 17, 2001, for the first time actual immigration records and ships' passenger manifests could be researched and viewed *online at no charge*. And it sure did create a sensation: The site was receiving 27,000 hits *per second*. U.S. News and World Report declared that the site, ". . . may well be the most popular launch in Internet history, eclipsing Madonna and the Beatles." And it's no wonder—40 percent of Americans today trace their roots back to an ancestor whose records are in the Ellis Island Database. And it appeared they were all trying to find those records at the same time!

Nearly four years later the site continues to be extremely popular. We have learned that research tools can always be improved. We have paid close attention to the feedback we have received from the millions of people who have used our Web site and have recently re-launched the site with improved navigation, retooled and advanced search capabilities, and a new genealogy learning center which offers research tips and free downloadable forms.

But genealogy is not an exact science and even with these great search tools and tips you can't always easily find your ancestor. And that's where Sharon DeBartolo Carmack comes in. We were pleased to have her serve on the Foundation's history committee during the planning stage for the Center and the site. And we are equally pleased with the tremendous genealogy tool she has created with *The Family Tree Guide to Finding Your Ellis Island Ancestors*. She provides everything from a primer for getting started on your family history quest to valuable tips and ingenious tricks for using the Ellis Island Database and the many other resources that are available.

The Family Tree Guide to Finding Your Ellis Island Ancestors provides a treasure trove of useful information to the over 100 million people whose family roots are waiting to be unearthed in the Ellis Island immigration records. My family came through Ellis Island and I know first hand the excitement of finding my mother's name on the manifest and having that visceral connection with my family's immigrant saga. This book will be a tremendous aid in bringing you to that exciting place of discovery. Happy digging!

Stephen A. Briganti
President and Chief Executive Officer
The Statue of Liberty-Ellis Island Foundation, Inc.

Introduction

More than twenty million passengers came through the Golden Door at Ellis Island, and statistics say that at least one of them might be your ancestor. It's estimated that about 40 percent of Americans has an ancestor who came through Ellis Island. Finding yours among the twenty-plus million, however, may be a challenge. Some of us are lucky enough to know the exact date of arrival or even the name of the ship our ancestors emigrated on. Unfortunately, many of us have sketchy information at best. For some, the "Island of Hope, Island of Tears" takes on a new meaning. If you've already been on the massive Ellis Island database, hoping that your ancestor's passenger arrival list was just a mouse click away, you may have quickly discovered that it wasn't going to be as easy as you thought. You don't need to dot and dash the distress signal for SOS; help has arrived.

Within these pages, you'll learn what basic information you need to know in order to find your ancestor on a passenger list, and how to make sure that you have the correct immigrant. You'll gain an understanding of how passenger lists were compiled, as it's important to know about a record's creation (and destruction; see Appendix A) in order to find elusive ancestors. The Ellis Island database is one of the highlights of online genealogy; this book will explain how the database was compiled in order to make your searches more efficient. If that still fails, we'll look at other databases that might help your search, as well as how to search for your ancestor's arrival the old-fashioned way: checking microfilmed indexes and corresponding microfilmed passenger lists.

While Ellis Island was the major immigrant receiving station of its day, Castle Garden predated it, opening in 1855. How do you find your Castle Garden immigrant ancestor? You'll find the help you need for that time period here, too. Then you'll explore the history of Ellis Island and how it came to be the busiest port of arrival for millions of people.

Once you find your ancestor's arrival, you may be curious about the immigrant experience. What was it like for your ancestor to leave his homeland, travel aboard a crowded steamship, then process through the busiest port and immigrant receiving center the world has ever known? Each immigrant had to pass many examinations, including some stringent medical ones. What happened if your ancestor was sick upon arrival? Where did your ancestor get medical treatment? You'll learn the whole immigrant experience in vivid detail, almost as if you were going through it yourself.

You may also want to know details about the ship your ancestor traveled on. How big was it? How fast did it travel? How many passengers could it hold? Many sources are available—both online and in print—to help you learn this information, and you may likely find a photograph of the ship.

Finally, after all the time you spent finding your Ellis Island ancestor and learning about the experiences your ancestor faced in order to come to this country, it would be a shame not to share it with other family members and future descendants. We'll look at several ways to preserve the Ellis Island experience of your ancestors for the future.

Your ancestors made a remarkable journey to get to this country. Now it's your turn to embark on a remarkable journey of your own—the Ellis Island journey. It's one you will enjoy and won't forget. Join me.

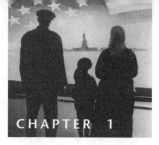

CHAPTER 1

Starting Your Ellis Island Search

hen the Ellis Island database made its debut on the Internet in April 2001, you may have been one of the millions anxious to do a search for your immigrant ancestor. Once you were able to get into the database—since it was overloaded for weeks—were you one of the lucky ones who was able to find your ancestor immediately? If so, congratulations! But if not and you're still scratching your head, trying to figure out why you can't find your ancestor, or you're trying to sort out which one of the hundreds of Patrick Doyles is yours, one roadblock may be that you don't know enough information about him to find him.

Although the database has transcription problems (which can necessitate some creative searching techniques; I'll detail more in chapter three), you need to know some basic information about your ancestor before you begin your search of passenger lists, whether it be online or on microfilm. **Here is what you must know to make your search successful:**

- The name your ancestor used in the Old Country
- Your ancestor's approximate age (or date of birth)
- The approximate date your ancestor arrived

Important

These additional details will help you in your search:

- The place your ancestor came from (last residence in the Old Country or place of birth)
- Who traveled with your ancestor to America

Now let's look at the three steps that will help you find this information about your ancestor:

1. Discovering the who, when, and where
2. Exploring records for clues
3. Unearthing the how, why, and what

STEP 1: DISCOVERING THE WHO, WHEN, AND WHERE

All genealogical research begins with the who, the when, and the where: the names of your ancestors, the dates of important events such as births, marriages, deaths, and immigration, and the places these events occurred. To successfully research any immigrant, you need to learn the immigrant's full original name, his approximate date of birth, and his place of birth. This information may be obtained from your research or from talking with relatives.

As you learn the who, when, and where, record this information. I recommend you use forms such as a *pedigree* or *ancestor chart* and a *family group sheet*. These forms may be downloaded for free from the Internet at various sites, including <www.familytreemagazine.com/forms>. Or you may want to purchase a genealogy computer software program, which will create the forms for you. You can find software programs at your local media store. Regardless of where you get the forms, make sure you record the sources of information as you gather facts.

WHEN DID THEY ARRIVE?

Just as it is sometimes impossible to determine an exact date of birth or death for some ancestors, it is also a grim reality that you may never find the exact date an ancestor arrived in America. The best you may be able to achieve is to narrow down an approximate time frame of arrival. This makes it all the more important to exhaust every possible record created by, for, or about your immigrant ancestors from the moment they stepped foot on American shores. By constructing a chronology of your ancestor's life in America based on your search, you'll be able to pinpoint, as close as possible, an approximate arrival time.

Talking to Relatives

Interviewing relatives can reveal valuable clues about your Ellis Island ancestors, clues that may make the difference between a successful search and one that produces nothing. You may even have a relative still alive who came through the Golden Door as a child, or more likely, the immigrant's children—who heard their parent's story over and over again. Being able to interview the immigrant or his children adds a great and unique advantage to your search. Someone with eighteenth-century or earlier immigrant ancestors can't do this! You are just a generation or two away from the Old Country and Ellis Island.

Oral History

Obviously, you want to get as many of the basic facts as you can.
- What was the name of the ship?
- When did Grandma arrive?

- Did she come through Ellis Island?
- How old was she when she came to this country?
- What was her name then?

But you also want to get their *stories* about the immigrant experience. (See chapter ten for information on Ellis Island's taped oral history collection.)

- Why did you leave your homeland?
- What was the ship like?
- Was it crowded?
- Were you scared? Anxious? Excited?
- Did you travel third class?
- Describe the journey for me.
- What was the processing like on Ellis Island?

Be aware that some of these immigration stories have gotten more "colorful" with each telling and with each generation that tells it. Almost all immigration stories have some grain of truth, as they are not usually created out of thin air. It's that tiny grain that may be the clue that leads you to genealogical success. Two common myths have worked their way into many immigrant family stories, and perhaps you've already heard one of these.

The Stowaway Myth

For some reason, it is so much more romantic to have an ancestor who came to America as a stowaway on a ship rather than a paying passenger. While some people actually did sneak aboard ships, this was not an overly common practice. Stowaways, if discovered, will be recorded on the passenger list on either the last page of the manifest or a free line of a page, typically with a notation saying "stowaway" or perhaps "SI," meaning they were held for Ellis Island's Board of Special Inquiry. Stowaways may also be recorded as crew members if the stowaway was discovered en route and put to work to earn his passage. (See chapter two, page 23 for more on searching for stowaways.) If you have the family story of a stowaway, still check for a passenger arrival list. But don't be surprised if your ancestor actually paid for passage.

The Ellis Island Baptism Myth

Ever heard that an immigrant ancestor's surname was changed by officials during processing at Ellis Island? This is one of the most persistent myths in genealogy. No evidence exists to suggest this ever occurred, although many descendants insist their ancestor's name was changed on Ellis Island and refuse to believe anything to the contrary. **If you talk with the historians at Ellis Island, they will tell you that names were not changed—the officials had no reason to do so—and that this is just a colorful family story.**

During its operation as an immigrant receiving station (1892–1954), Ellis

Important

Island was staffed with hundreds of interpreters who spoke more than thirty different languages. Inspectors compared the names the immigrants told them against what was recorded on the passenger lists, which were created at the port of departure. The inspectors were not allowed to make changes to the list. Additionally, the inspectors had no reason to change anyone's surname once they arrived on the island. Often, after immigrants settled in America they changed their own names to avoid prejudice and to blend more easily into American society. Another typical time for forenames, and sometimes surnames, to be changed was when immigrant children entered school, and American teachers could not pronounce the foreign names. So they called Francesco "Frank," and Adamczyk became "Adams."

Historian Marian L. Smith of the U.S. Citizenship and Immigration Services in Washington, D.C., wrote an informative article: "American Names / Declaring Independence," <http://uscis.gov/graphics/aboutus/history/articles/nameessay.html>. In the article, she states that "the Ellis-Island-name-change-story . . . is as American as apple pie," but the facts of immigrant processing just did not allow for names to be changed on Ellis Island. So in order to find your ancestors on passenger lists, you will need to know the original name your ancestor went by in the homeland. The name your ancestor gave when purchasing the ticket to America will be the name that will be recorded on the list. But just like any document, the name could have been accidentally misspelled, or the name could appear to be spelled a different way because of the clerk's handwriting; an *a* looks like an *o* or an *e*, for example.

How Family Stories Can Help

Every time I interviewed my mother, she insisted that her mother, Rose (Norris) Gordon, was born in Ireland. The family story she remembered was that Rose had contracted scarlet fever on board the ship. I knew this couldn't be right; I had Rose's birth certificate and she was the youngest of seven children, all born in Greenwich, Connecticut. Even though I knew that every family story usually contains a grain of truth, I shrugged this one off as the exception to the rule—until many years later when I interviewed my mother's older sister. She told me that the family had gone back to Ireland after Rose was born, and on the return trip, Rose had scarlet fever.

On my next trip to the Family History Library in Salt Lake City, Utah, I couldn't wait to look at the microfilm of passenger lists to see if I could verify the story. (This was before the release of the Ellis Island database online.) Sure enough, I found the whole family—all U.S. citizens—returning from Ireland on the *Oceanic* on 31 October 1901 (the day after Rose turned five) and docking at the Port of New York. The ship's manifest showed no indication, however, that Rose had been sick.

In finding the ship's list, I also had another breakthrough on this family.

Rose's father, according to his death certificate, was supposedly born in County Tyrone, Northern Ireland, but without a more precise location such as a town or parish I was unable to pursue research in Ireland. On the passenger list, however, the family's last residence was listed as Cookstown. Ireland has several Cookstowns, including one in County Tyrone. Not long after, I was able to identify the townland near Cookstown where the family originated.

Although my mother didn't have all the facts straight, her older sister had remembered the story with more accuracy. In all the documents I had collected on this family, nothing indicated that they were ever out of the country once the parents came here originally. So I learned a valuable lesson: Never ignore a family story no matter how far-fetched it may seem at the time. Had I not tried to verify my mother's version of the story with my aunt, I would have never dreamed of looking for the family on a passenger list—and I would have missed the clue that led me to my great-grandfather's origins in Ireland.

Home Sources

While you are interviewing your relatives, **don't forget to ask to see artifacts, photographs, and documents that might aid in your search.** Grandma may have had to leave everything behind in Greece, but she just couldn't part with her mother's silver candlesticks, which she brought with her. Is a date, craftsman, or place engraved on the bottom? Will that lead you to a village of origin? Examine thoroughly every artifact that may have come from the Old Country or that was acquired upon arrival in America. Study family photographs. Were they taken here or in the homeland? You may find in the family photograph collection a postcard depicting the native village or the ship your ancestor arrived on. On family or individual portraits, the photographer may have imprinted his name and locality on the front or back. Analyze all photographs and artifacts for possible clues.

Hidden Treasures

Figure 1-1
Angelina (Vallarelli) Ebetino, who immigrated from Italy to America in 1910, brought this coffee pot and matching dishware with her.

For More Info

See Maureen Taylor's *Uncovering Your Ancestry through Family Photographs,* 2d ed. (Cincinnati: Family Tree Books, 2005).

Ask relatives if they possess any of these documents:
- Citizenship papers
- Passports
- Alien registration cards
- Steamship ticket stubs
- Journals or diaries
- U.S. Public Health Service inspection cards from the ship
- Letters or documents written in a foreign language
- Military discharge certificates
- Newspaper clippings

STEP 2: EXPLORING RECORDS FOR CLUES

Throughout most of U.S. history, the federal government created records to keep track of foreign nationals entering and residing in America, primarily naturalization records and passenger arrival lists. While you no doubt want to jump right to passenger arrival lists, remember, unless you know the date of arrival and name of the ship, you won't get very far. You need to get that information from somewhere, especially when you are searching in the busiest port in American history.

Naturalization Records

Depending on the time of your ancestor's immigration, naturalization records can give you the precise date and port of arrival, as well as the name of the ship, the port of departure, and the immigrant's date and place of birth. Some records, however, may give you only the year when the immigrant arrived. Regardless, the naturalization record is worth seeking for any and all information it may give you. Although the early naturalization laws won't apply to your Ellis Island search, an overview of the history is helpful. For more detailed coverage, see John J. Newman's *American Naturalization Processes and Procedures, 1790–1985* (Indianapolis: Indiana Historical Society, 1985; reprint: Bountiful, Utah: Heritage Quest, 1998) and Loretto Dennis Szucs's *They Became Americans: Finding Naturalization Records and Ethnic Origins* (Salt Lake City: Ancestry Inc., 1998).

Between 1776 and 1790, each state established its own laws, procedures, and residency requirements for aliens to become naturalized citizens. After 1790, when the first federal naturalization law was passed, a series of acts changed restrictions and requirements for the whole country over the centuries.

In 1790, the applicant for citizenship had to be a free white male, twenty-one years of age or older, who had lived in the United States for two years and in the state in which he applied for one year. The applicant could have applied in any court of public record—federal, state, or local—in any one of the states.

In 1795, a two-step process was created for applicants to gain U.S. citizenship.

First, a declaration of intention needed to be filed, then a minimum of three years later the alien could petition for naturalization (see Figures 1-2, below, and 1-3 on page 10). At that time, eligibility was extended to free white females at least twenty-one years old, and the United States residency requirement was raised to five years. In 1798, the residency requirement was extended to fourteen years. In 1801, it was reduced back to five years, where it has remained since.

The 1795 law stipulated that applicants had to declare their intent at least three years prior to naturalization; in 1824, this requirement was amended to two years. The 1824 law also stipulated that the naturalization process could be effected in one step if the applicant was under the age of eighteen when he or she immigrated and had resided in the United States for three full years before turning twenty-one and petitioning for citizenship. This was known as "minor naturalization."

A nationality act of 1870, approved on July 14 of that year, allowed for naturalization of those of African nativity or descent, although ratification of the Fourteenth Amendment to the U.S. Constitution in 1868 had made former slaves citizens. Asians could not become American citizens from 1882 until 1943. Copies of alien naturalization files, known as the "A-Files" (1943 to the present), are held by the U.S. Citizenship and Immigration Services. They may be obtained through a Freedom of Information/Privacy Act request, using Form G-639 (see page 13 on how to obtain records). In 1910, Asian Indians were

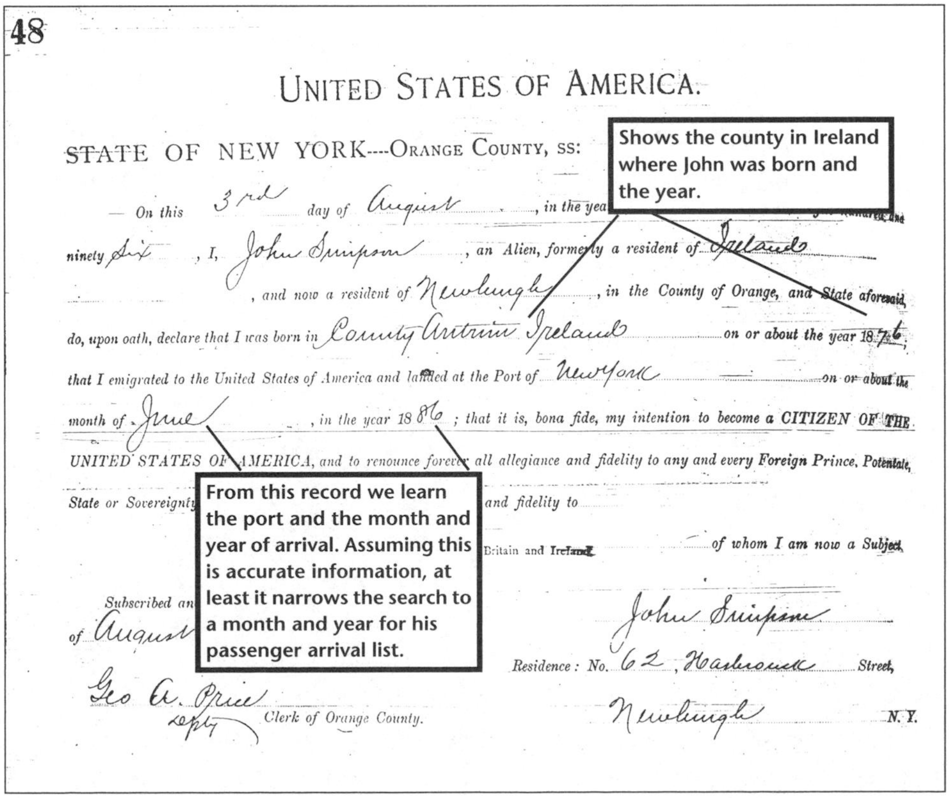
48

UNITED STATES OF AMERICA.

STATE OF NEW YORK----ORANGE COUNTY, ss:

— On this 3rd day of August, in the yea[r] ... hundred and ninety Six, I, John Simpson, an Alien, formerly a resident of Ireland, and now a resident of Newburgh, in the County of Orange, and State aforesaid, do, upon oath, declare that I was born in County Antrim Ireland on or about the year 1876; that I emigrated to the United States of America and landed at the Port of New York on or about the month of June, in the year 1886; that it is, bona fide, my intention to become a CITIZEN OF THE UNITED STATES OF AMERICA, and to renounce forever all allegiance and fidelity to any and every Foreign Prince, Potentate, State or Sovereignty ... and fidelity to ... Britain and Ireland of whom I am now a Subject.

Subscribed an[d] ... of August ...

John Simpson

Residence: No. 62, Hasbrouck Street, Newburgh N.Y.

Geo A. Price, Depty Clerk of Orange County.

Figure 1-2
Declaration of intention for John Simpson, Orange County, New York, FHL 1298783, item 5, 1895–1906. Pre-1906 naturalization records give only scanty information.

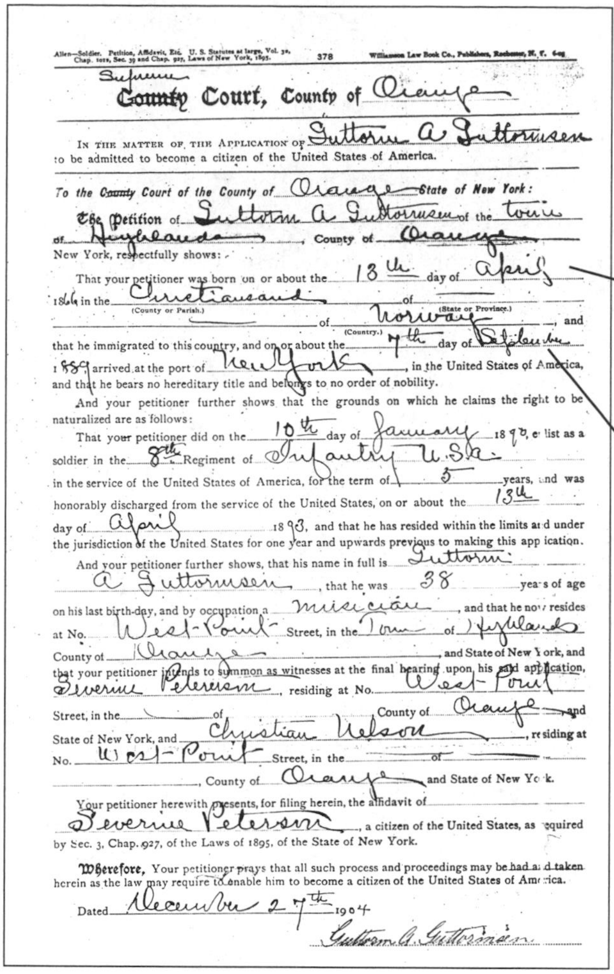

Figure 1-3
Petition for naturalization of Guttorm A. Guttormsen, Orange County, New York, FHL 1298782.

Gives the petitioner's date and place of birth.

Gives the date and port of arrival.

eligible for a short time, however, the Supreme Court ruled them ineligible in 1923. Filipinos and Asian Indians were banned from citizenship until 1946. Laws passed in 1887 and 1924 made American Indians citizens.

Prior to 1903 some courts did not have an applicant file a petition (application) for naturalization, though it was required. A form was created in 1903 by the U.S. Department of Justice specifically for this purpose, but not all courts used it. The nineteenth-century records may contain some or all of the following data: the applicant's name, country of birth, date of application, and signature. Some give the date and port of arrival, occupation, residence, age, birthplace, and date of birth.

As every bureaucratic process has loopholes, people found ways to avoid legally becoming a citizen. For example, a person might obtain several copies of his declaration and then sell them at election time, so aliens could vote. Also, more aliens applied at county and state courts than federal because the fee was usually less and standards may not have been as stringent.

The Bureau of Immigration and Naturalization—known as the **Immigration and Naturalization Service** for a time and now known as the **U.S. Citizenship and Immigra-**

Notes

tion Services <www.uscis.gov>—was established in 1906, and copies of all naturalizations made after this date in courts around the country were forwarded to that agency. Becoming a naturalized citizen became standardized and involved the process of filing a declaration of intention (first papers), then after fulfilling the residency requirement, filing a petition for naturalization, which required the applicant's signature (second or final papers).

In the first papers, or declaration of intention, an alien renounced his allegiance to his homeland and declared his intention to become a U.S. citizen. The declaration needed to be submitted between two and seven years before the petition. Post-1906 declarations of intention include the applicant's name, age, occupation, and personal description; date and place of birth; citizenship; present address and last foreign address; vessel and port of embarkation; U.S. port and date of arrival; date of application; and signature (see Figure 1-4 below).

In the naturalization petition (second or final papers), an immigrant who had already filed the intention papers and had met the residency requirements made a formal application for citizenship (see Figure 1-5 on page 12). Infor-

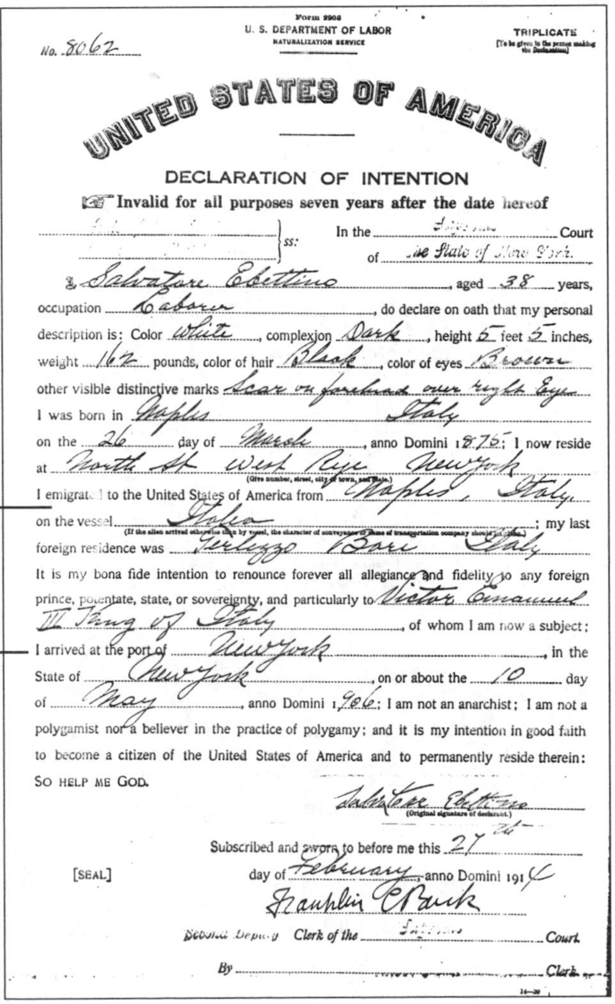

Figure 1-4
Declaration of intention for Salvatore Ebetino, 27 February 1914, case number 8062, Supreme Court of New York, Westchester County; Westchester County Records Center and Archives, Elmsford, New York.

Gives the port of departure and the name of the vessel.

Gives the port of arrival and the date.

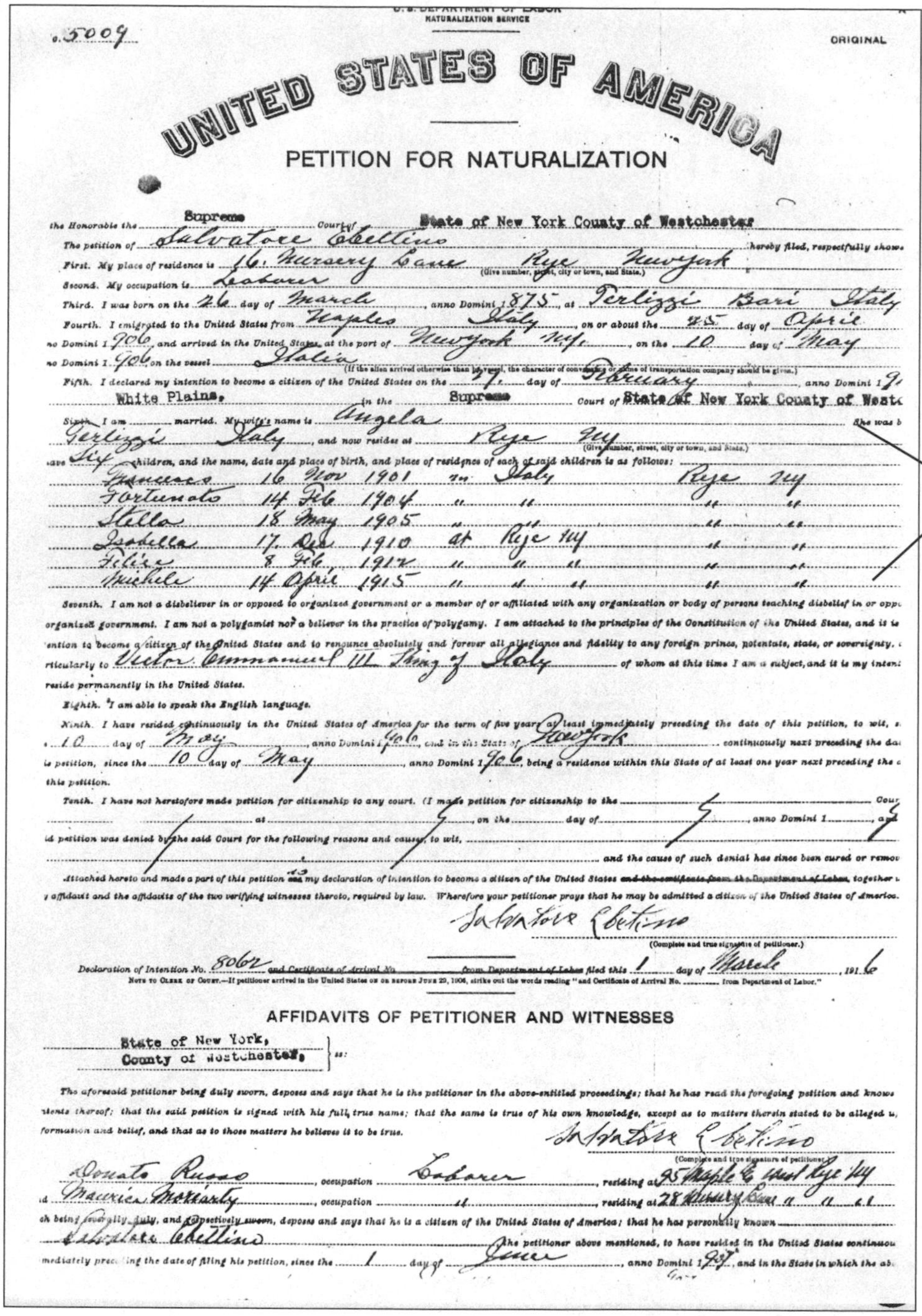
U.S. DEPARTMENT OF LABOR
NATURALIZATION SERVICE

No. 5009 ORIGINAL

UNITED STATES OF AMERICA

PETITION FOR NATURALIZATION

To the Honorable the Supreme Court of State of New York County of Westchester

The petition of Salvatore Ebetino hereby filed, respectfully shows:

First. My place of residence is 16 Nursery Lane Rye New York (Give number, street, city or town, and State.)

Second. My occupation is Laborer

Third. I was born on the 26 day of March, anno Domini 1875, at Terlizzi Bari Italy

Fourth. I emigrated to the United States from Naples Italy, on or about the 25 day of April, anno Domini 1906, and arrived in the United States, at the port of New York NY, on the 10 day of May, anno Domini 1906 on the vessel Italia (If the alien arrived otherwise than by vessel, the character of conveyance or name of transportation company should be given.)

Fifth. I declared my intention to become a citizen of the United States on the 27 day of February, anno Domini 19.. White Plains, in the Supreme Court of State of New York County of Westc...

Sixth. I am married. My wife's name is Angela. She was b... Terlizzi Italy, and now resides at Rye NY (Give number, street, city or town, and State.)

...have Six children, and the name, date and place of birth, and place of residence of each of said children is as follows:

Francesco	16 Nov 1901	in Italy	Rye NY
Fortunato	14 Feb 1904	" "	" "
Stella	18 May 1905	" "	" "
Isabella	17 Dec 1910	at Rye NY	" "
Felice	8 Feb 1912	" " "	" "
Michele	14 April 1915	" " "	" "

Seventh. I am not a disbeliever in or opposed to organized government or a member of or affiliated with any organization or body of persons teaching disbelief in or opp... organized government. I am not a polygamist nor a believer in the practice of polygamy. I am attached to the principles of the Constitution of the United States, and it is ...ention to become a citizen of the United States and to renounce absolutely and forever all allegiance and fidelity to any foreign prince, potentate, state, or sovereignty, ...rticularly to Victor Emmanuel III King of Italy of whom at this time I am a subject, and it is my inten... reside permanently in the United States.

Eighth. I am able to speak the English language.

Ninth. I have resided continuously in the United States of America for the term of five years at least immediately preceding the date of this petition, to wit, ... 10 day of May, anno Domini 1906, and in the State of New York continuously next preceding the da... ...is petition, since the 10 day of May, anno Domini 1906, being a residence within this State of at least one year next preceding the ... this petition.

Tenth. I have not heretofore made petition for citizenship to any court. (I made petition for citizenship to the ... Cou... at ..., on the ... day of ..., anno Domini 1..., and ...id petition was denied by the said Court for the following reasons and causes, to wit, ... and the cause of such denial has since been cured or remov...

Attached hereto and made a part of this petition are my declaration of intention to become a citizen of the United States ~~and the certificate from the Department of Labor~~, together ... affidavit and the affidavits of the two verifying witnesses thereto, required by law. Wherefore your petitioner prays that he may be admitted a citizen of the United States of America.

Salvatore Ebetino
(Complete and true signature of petitioner.)

Declaration of Intention No. 8062 ~~and Certificate of Arrival No. ... from Department of Labor~~ filed this 1 day of March, 1916

Note to Clerk of Court.—If petitioner arrived in the United States on or before June 29, 1906, strike out the words reading "and Certificate of Arrival No. ... from Department of Labor."

AFFIDAVITS OF PETITIONER AND WITNESSES

State of New York, County of Westchester } ss:

The aforesaid petitioner being duly sworn, deposes and says that he is the petitioner in the above-entitled proceedings; that he has read the foregoing petition and knows ...ntents thereof; that the said petition is signed with his full, true name; that the same is true of his own knowledge, except as to matters therein stated to be alleged u... ...formation and belief, and that as to those matters he believes it to be true.

Salvatore Ebetino
(Complete and true signature of petitioner.)

Donato Russo, occupation Laborer, residing at 95 Maple Av West Rye NY
...d Maurice Moriarty, occupation ", residing at 28 Nursery Lane " " "
...ch being severally, duly, and respectively sworn, deposes and says that he is a citizen of the United States of America; that he has personally known Salvatore Ebetino the petitioner above mentioned, to have resided in the United States continuou... ...mediately preceding the date of filing his petition, since the 1 day of June, anno Domini 1907, and in the State in which the ab...

Figure 1-5
Petition for naturalization for Salvatore Ebetino, 1 March 1916, number 5009, Supreme Court of New York, Westchester County; Westchester County Records Center and Archives, Elmsford, New York.

Before 1922, women and children became citizens when the husband/father did, so you may find information about the petitioner's wife and children.

mation on the petition includes name, residence, occupation, date and place of birth, citizenship, and personal description of applicant; date of emigration; ports of embarkation and arrival; marital status (with wife's name and date of birth, if married); names, dates, places of birth, and residence of applicant's children; date at which U.S. residence commenced; time of residence in state; name changes; and signature. After 1929, photographs were included on the declaration and final certificate. In the deposition that accompanied the petition, witnesses signed in support of the applicant.

The naturalization law of 1906 stated that, after the petition had been filed, a ninety-day waiting period followed before the hearing and citizenship was granted or denied. Also no naturalization hearings occurred thirty days prior to any general election within the court's area of jurisdiction. The new U.S. citizen was given a certificate of citizenship bearing the seal of the naturalizing court. This document may be preserved and handed down from generation to generation in many American families.

Between 1855 and 1922, an alien wife automatically became a citizen when her husband did or when she married an American citizen. This was called "derivative" citizenship. Conversely, a congressional act of 1907 declared that if an American woman married an alien, she lost her citizenship and took on the nationality of her husband. She was then no longer eligible for U.S. citizenship unless her husband applied and was accepted. After 1922, the law was changed to allow women to obtain citizenship independently, and they did not lose it when they married aliens. Since the first federal naturalization law of 1790, children (under the age of twenty-one) enjoyed derivative citizenship when the father became naturalized.

CAN'T FIND HIS NATURALIZATION?

Members of some ethnic groups—Italians, Greeks, and Poles—were slow to become naturalized, if they did at all, or were not allowed to do so. Typically, those men who were "birds of passage" did not rush to become American citizens. In many cases, their goal was not to settle permanently in America; it was to earn money and return to their homeland and buy land there. Birds of passage were those who went back and forth between countries, working for a time in one country, then returning to their homeland. This may be a reason you can't find a naturalization record for your ancestor, or you find one several years after your ancestor arrived.

For More Info

For more on laws affecting the citizenship of women, see Marian L. Smith, "Women and Naturalization, ca. 1802–1940," in *Prologue* 30 (Summer 1998): 146-153.

Obtaining Naturalization Records

To obtain naturalization records, check at the courthouses—municipal, county, state, and federal—where the immigrant arrived and/or settled. These records may have also been microfilmed by the Family History Library, as well as any indexes to the records that may exist. Also check city, county, and state archives. Naturalizations made in municipal courts may be found in the town halls or city archives of some major cities, such as Baltimore, Chicago, and St. Louis. And as I mentioned, copies of all naturalizations after 1906 are on file with the U.S. Citizenship and Immigration Services (USCIS). If these avenues fail, send a letter with the immigrant's name, date of birth, and place of birth to the USCIS office in the state where your ancestor was naturalized. Go to <http://uscis.gov/graphics/abo utus/foia/address.htm> for a directory. If you don't know in which state your ancestor was naturalized, write to the USCIS office nearest your place of residence. You'll be making your request under the Freedom of Information Act <http://uscis.gov/graphics/aboutus/foia/request.htm>.

Certificates of Arrival

Between 1906 and the early 1940s, the Bureau of Immigration and Naturalization (i.e., INS or USCIS) may have created a certificate of arrival for your ancestor. These certificates were created when an applicant applied for citizenship and officials checked the ship's manifest to verify legal admission. If the arrival record was found, the INS (USCIS) issued a certificate of arrival and sent it back to the court where the alien applied for citizenship. This certificate, if created and extant, should be on file with the naturalization record. It will list the port of entry, the date, and the name of the ship. You may also find a manifest number, such as 1-39-5235, giving the list number, group number, and volume number of the manifest. (See chapters two and four for details on finding and using ship's manifests, or passenger lists.)

Naturalization Stub Books

Although largely unindexed and arranged by filing date, surviving naturalization certificate stub books are another useful source. Most courts did not keep a copy of the naturalization certificate given to the new citizen, but they may have retained the "stubs" attached to the certificates that were bound in volumes. While these records vary in content over the years and from one court to another, they may contain the date the alien declared his intention to become a citizen, his age, and the names and ages of his wife and children. Look for these stub books in the courts of various jurisdictions that handled naturalizations and in archives and historical societies.

Alien Registrations

Aliens were required to register their current addresses and places of employment with the federal government between 1940 and about 1982. The Alien Registration Act of 1940 required aliens to report their address and employment and to report any change of address immediately. In 1952, this changed to reporting their address annually. The address reporting ended in the 1980s, and only the last/most recent address might remain on file (see Figure 1-6 on page 15). Requests for alien registration information may be made to the Director, Freedom of Information Act/Privacy Act Program, U.S. Citizenship and Immigration Services, 425 I Street, Northwest, Second Floor, ULLICO Building, Washington, D.C. 20536. Alien registration cards may often be found among family papers and keepsakes.

Notes

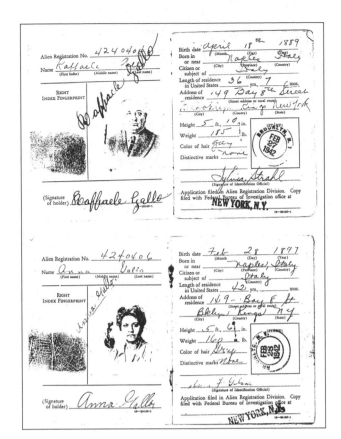

Visas and Passports

Records of the Visa Office from 1910 to 1940 are open to the public. They are located in National Archives II in College Park, Maryland <www.archives .gov/facilities/index.html>. The records are arranged chronologically in ten-year groupings, then alphabetically by surname.

Except for brief periods during wartime, 19 August 1861 to 17 March 1862 and 22 May 1918 to 1921 (the Civil War and World War I), passports were not required of U.S. citizens who traveled out of the country prior to 1941. Many Americans, however, for their own security, obtained them. Passports were, and still are, issued by the U.S. Department of State, and those issued from 1791 to 1925 have been transferred to the National Archives. The originals are housed at the National Archives II, College Park, Maryland. They are on microfilm and have indexes and registers to help you find them. The Family History Library also has this microfilm. Go to the FamilySearch site <www.familysearch.org>, click on "Search the Family History Library Catalog for records and resources," then search by subject on "passports." Click on those for the United States.

Applications contain little information, but from 1906 to 1925, they included the name of the applicant, date and place of birth, name and date and place of birth of spouse or children, residence and occupation at the time of

Figure 1-7
Application for a passport for Merchol Fee, 1 December 1877, NARA microfilm M1372, roll 220, volume 487, number 3869.

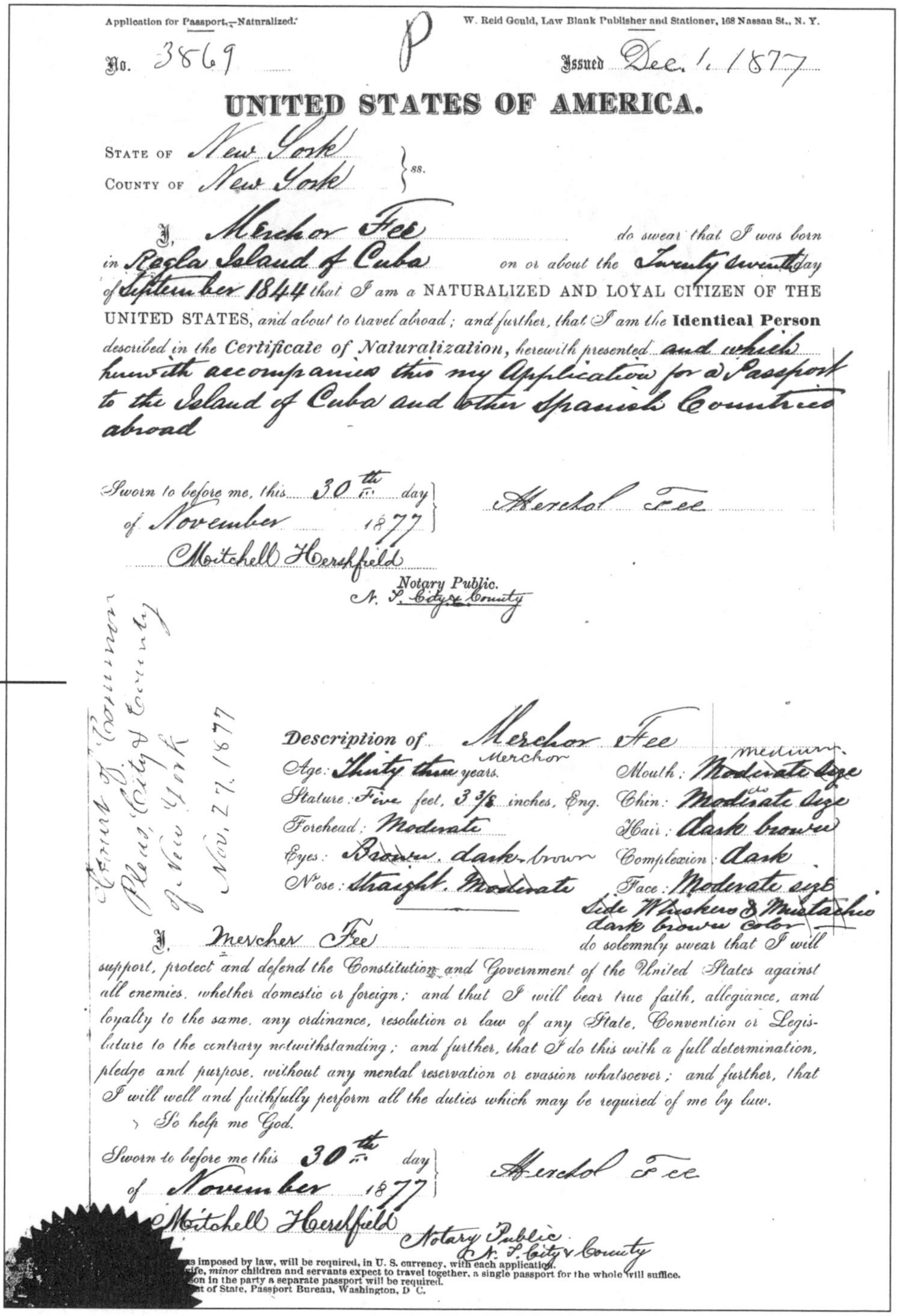
Application for Passport,—Naturalized. W. Reid Gould, Law Blank Publisher and Stationer, 168 Nassau St., N. Y.

No. 3869 P Issued Dec. 1, 1877

UNITED STATES OF AMERICA.

STATE OF New York } ss.
COUNTY OF New York }

I, Merchor Fee do swear that I was born in Regla Island of Cuba on or about the Twenty seventh day of September 1844 that I am a NATURALIZED AND LOYAL CITIZEN OF THE UNITED STATES, and about to travel abroad; and further, that I am the Identical Person described in the Certificate of Naturalization, herewith presented and which herewith accompanies this my Application for a Passport to the Island of Cuba and other Spanish Countries abroad

Sworn to before me, this 30th day of November 1877 — Merchol Fee
Mitchell Hershfield, Notary Public. N. Y. City & County

Court of Common Pleas, City & County of New York, Nov. 27, 1877

Description of Merchor Fee (Merchor)
Age: Thirty three years. Mouth: Moderate size (medium)
Stature: Five feet, 3 3/8 inches, Eng. Chin: Moderate size
Forehead: Moderate Hair: dark brown
Eyes: Brown, dark brown Complexion: dark
Nose: Straight, Moderate Face: Moderate size
Side Whiskers & Mustachio dark brown color

I, Merchor Fee do solemnly swear that I will support, protect and defend the Constitution and Government of the United States against all enemies, whether domestic or foreign; and that I will bear true faith, allegiance, and loyalty to the same, any ordinance, resolution or law of any State, Convention or Legislature to the contrary notwithstanding; and further, that I do this with a full determination, pledge and purpose, without any mental reservation or evasion whatsoever; and further, that I will well and faithfully perform all the duties which may be required of me by law. So help me God.

Sworn to before me this 30th day of November 1877 — Merchol Fee
Mitchell Hershfield, Notary Public, N. Y. City & County

...s imposed by law, will be required, in U. S. currency, with each application. ...ife, minor children and servants expect to travel together, a single passport for the whole will suffice. ...on in the party a separate passport will be required. ...t of State, Passport Bureau, Washington, D. C.

Written on the side of this document is the court in which he became naturalized and the date (Court of Common Pleas, City & County of New York, 27 November 1877).

application, immediate travel plans, physical description, and a photograph (see Figure 1-7 above). Passport applications of naturalized citizens included information about their immigration and naturalization, plus the date and port of arrival, name of ship, and the date and court of naturalization.

For passports after 1925, write to the Department of State, Passport Services, Research and Liaison Section, Room 500, 1111 Nineteenth Street,

Northwest, Washington, D.C. 20524-1705. If the applicant for the passport is still alive, you will need a letter from the applicant; if the person is deceased, you need to provide a copy of the death certificate and state your relationship to the deceased.

STEP 3: UNEARTHING THE WHY, HOW, AND WHAT

The trend in genealogy has shifted dramatically in the past decade or two. No longer are most genealogists satisfied with just names, dates, and places (the who, where, and when). They want to go beyond a skeletal pedigree chart to seek the person behind the name—to know *what* it was like to be an immigrant, *how* their ancestors came to this country, and *why*. Genealogical records do not ordinarily tell this information. Traditional genealogical documents—censuses, probates, land records, and so forth—tend to leave gaps in the immigrants' stories, no matter when they arrived. In order to supplement information found in records of individuals, we need to study the broader, common experiences, the day-to-day activities, and the folkways of the ethnic group. Naming, inheritance, marriage, religion, and migration patterns are all revealing and important to family historians. Learning these details can guide your research in the right direction and help you determine ethnic identity and immigrant origins.

While each group has it own traditions, customs, and immigration experiences, two factors are common to all immigrants, no matter when they arrived in America or what the ethnic background:

- Upon arrival, free people initially settled with friends and relatives from their homeland.
- The first generation typically tried to maintain as many of their native customs (folkways) as American society would allow.

Despite what we may have been taught in history classes, our immigrant ancestors were not always eager to adopt the traits of the dominant culture, nor did they all willingly come to America. **Logically, therefore, in order to identify immigrants and their origins, two research strategies apply:**

- Study the neighborhood and community. Who were your ancestor's neighbors and where did they come from? Your ancestors may not have left evidence suggesting their origins, but their neighbors and other associates could have.
- Study the social history to learn the folkways and common experiences of the ethnic group. If all the genealogical records state only that your ancestor was German or came from Germany, a study of social history in conjunction with the specific genealogical data will be necessary to determine whether the heritage was German, Alsatian, Swiss, Luxembourger, Russian, Austrian, or Prussian. In American records, these

Research Tip

groups were generally classified by the language they spoke—their mother tongue. If they spoke German, they were Germans. This dilemma is not exclusive to Germans, of course; although they are one of the most troublesome groups in genealogical research, other groups have similar identity problems in records.

Your research in social histories should be ongoing. As soon as you learn a possible ethnic identity, look for social histories for that group. Social histories discuss the everyday lives and cultures of ordinary people in society. For example, if you have Irish ancestors, a good social history would be Kerby A. Miller's *Emigrants and Exiles: Ireland and the Irish Exodus to North America* (New York: Oxford University Press, 1985); Italian ancestors, try Jerre Mangione and Ben Morreale's *La Storia: Five Centuries of the Italian American Experience* (New York: HarperCollins, 1992); or if you have Polish ancestors, look for John J. Bukowczyk's *And My Children Did Not Know Me: A History of the Polish-Americans* (Bloomington: Indiana University Press, 1987). Also look for children's books about the ethnic group to learn more about cultural traits. In particular, Chelsea House Publishers in Pennsylvania has produced two excellent series: the Peoples of North America, covering forty-nine ethnic groups, and Indians of North America, covering forty-nine tribes. These books are a quick read and provide a concise overview of the ethnic group's culture, migration and settlement patterns, and a bibliography of adult sources.

Continue your social history research while you are conducting interviews and examining original documents. If you have not studied the general, common immigration experiences and folkways of your immigrant ancestor's ethnic group, you may miss some important clues given in genealogical records, or you might overlook records that will yield more information.

HOW SOCIAL HISTORIES CAN HELP

When I began looking for Albino DeBartolo in the New York passenger arrival index, I found three entries for a man by that name. One arrived in 1905, another in 1909, and a third in 1912. Once I examined each passenger list, I discovered that each arrival was for the same man. Why was he going back and forth between Italy and America? By reading social histories of Italian Americans, I discovered he was a bird of passage (see "Can't Find His Naturalization" on page 13). This explained his behavior.

Once you've learned something about your immigrant ancestor and the social history of your ethnic heritage, it's time to move on to learning about passenger lists, so you can successfully find your ancestors.

CHAPTER 2

Passenger Lists 101

ere's today's riddle: What's the difference between a good researcher and a successful researcher? The good researcher knows how to find, search, and use records. The successful researcher also knows something about how and why the records (and their indexes) were created. You don't need to become an expert in the history of a particular record, but knowing the original purpose of records will help you understand why you may be having trouble finding your ancestor in a document or an index, and in turn, overcome that problem. While we would all like to think that the ship's purser was thinking, "I'd better get this guy's name spelled correctly, because one of his descendants is going to be hunting for him one hundred years from now," I'm afraid he had other things on his mind when he recorded your ancestor's name on the passenger manifest. So let's look at what you can expect to find and the reason some passenger lists give you more information than others.

SHIPS' MANIFESTS: THE BASICS

The federal government did not begin keeping a record of passenger arrivals until 1820, after Congress passed the Steerage Act in 1819, which regulated passenger travel and required ships' captains to keep a record of arriving immigrants. (Pre-1820 passenger lists were created by state or local authorities, and many have been published in a multitude of works. See Colletta's *They Came in Ships*.) Initially, captains used forms called Customs Lists, followed by another form called Immigration Passenger Lists. (The terms manifests and passenger lists are used here interchangeably.)

Customs Lists (1820–ca. 1891)

Passenger lists from 1820 to about 1891 were known as Customs Lists (see Figure 2-1 on page 20). They were usually printed in the United States, com-

For More Info

For more information on ship's lists, see John Colletta's *They Came in Ships* (Orem, Utah: Ancestry Inc., 2002) and Michael Tepper's *American Passenger Arrival Records* (Baltimore: Genealogical Publishing Co., 1993).

pleted by ship company personnel at the port of departure, and maintained primarily for statistical purposes; therefore, they contain scanty information: name of ship and its master, port of embarkation, date and port of arrival, and each passenger's name, sex, age, occupation, and nationality. Genealogists who have New York arrivals during this time might refer to these by the nickname of "Castle Garden lists" to distinguish them from the lists created during the Ellis Island years. (See chapter six.)

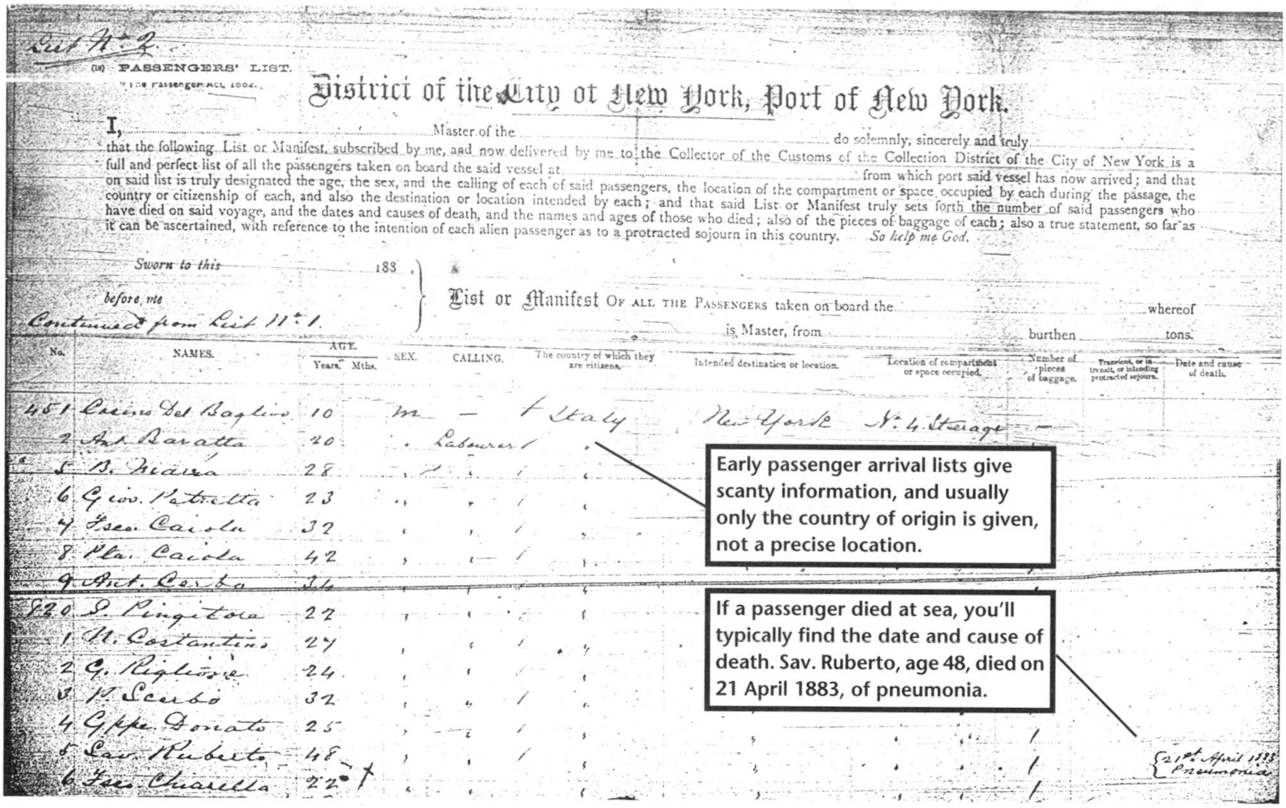

Figure 2-1
Customs list, *Utopia*, arriving at the Port of New York, 23 April 1883, NARA microfilm M237, roll 464.

Immigration Passenger Lists (ca. 1891–1954)

Arrival records created from about 1891 to the 1950s are called Immigration Passenger Lists (but genealogists with Ellis Island ancestors sometimes call them the "Ellis Island passenger lists"). Like Customs Lists, Immigration Passenger Lists were printed in the United States but completed at the port of departure, then filed in America after the ship docked. The information provided on Immigration Passenger Lists varied over the decades. As the influx of immigrants became greater, more details were recorded. For example, in 1893, the lists included twenty-one columns of information; in 1906, twenty-eight; in 1907, twenty-nine; and in 1917, thirty-three.

All the details you'll find on a passenger list are valuable to your research, but in particular, items such as last residence, final destination in the United States, if they're joining a relative and that relative's name and address, personal description, place of birth, and name and address of closest living relative in the native country will give you information you may not find anywhere else.

Finding the Lists

Most original passenger arrival lists, 1820–1957 (with some gaps), have been micro-filmed and are available at a number of repositories:

Microfilm Source

- National Archives and Records Administration (NARA) in Washington, D.C. The guide *Immigrant and Passenger Arrivals: A Select Catalog of National Archives Microfilm Publications* details more fully the availability of records and indexes for each port. This catalog is available on the Internet via the National Archives' Web site at <www.archives.gov/publicati ons/microfilm_catalogs/immigrant/immigrant_passenger_arrivals.html>.
- NARA regional records facilities with ports in their jurisdiction (i.e., NARA's Northeast Region in New York City has the lists for the Port of New York).
- Family History Library in Salt Lake City, Utah.
- Family History Centers worldwide. (You will have to order the microfilm for a small fee. For a center near you, go to <www.familysearch.org>.)

New York passenger lists are also available online:

- Ellis Island Database, New York Passenger Lists, 1892–1924 <www.elli sisland.org>. This is a free database, but you must pay to obtain a copy of the list. (See chapter three.)
- Ancestry.com's U.S. Immigration Collection, New York Passenger Lists, 1851–1891 <www.ancestry.com>. This is a subscription database. (See chapter six for more on these lists and arrivals at Castle Garden.)

Getting Copies of the Lists

Prints of microfilmed passenger lists may be obtained in a variety of ways:

- By visiting the National Archives in Washington, D.C., or NARA's Northeast Region facility in New York City. At these repositories, you can make prints from passenger list microfilms.
- By mail from the National Archives for a modest fee, using NATF Form 81. Forms may be requested online <www.archives.gov/global_pages/inqui re_form.html> or by letter to National Archives and Records Administration, 8601 Adelphi Road, College Park, Maryland 20740-6001. (You can also find the forms at NARA regional records services facilities.) The National Archives will not do research for you, however. The minimum information required for a search of the index is (1) full name of the person, (2) port of arrival, and (3) the month and year of arrival. Additional facts, such as the passenger's age and names of accompanying passengers, are

also helpful. If the list is not indexed, more specific information is needed, such as the exact date of arrival and the name of the ship.

- By visiting the Family History Library in Salt Lake City, Utah, or ordering the microfilm at one of the Family History Centers. At these repositories, you can make prints from microfilms yourself.
- By ordering a print of the passenger list from the Ellis Island Web site <www.ellisisland.org>.
- By printing out on your home printer passenger lists off the Ancestry .com site. (Remember, this is a subscription site and the New York lists cover only 1851–1891.)

SHIP'S MANIFESTS IN MORE DETAIL

Tip

When you find your ancestor's name on a passenger arrival list, of course you will make or obtain a copy of the list, but you'll also want to copy the information into your notes. (See Appendix B for transcription forms.) **By transcribing this information exactly as written into your notes, you will notice more details than you would just by looking at it.** You might notice abbreviations or numbers by your ancestor's name or by the name of someone who accompanied them. These notations can reveal more about your ancestor and may lead you to additional records.

Births, Deaths, and Marriages at Sea

All his life, Albert Trimigliozzi believed he was born in Norwich, Connecticut, on 24 January 1913. He even had a birth certificate to prove it. The problem was his parents hadn't arrived in America until five days after his birth, on 29 January 1913. On the passenger arrival list, next to his parents' names, are a few indiscernible cryptic notations, but nothing to indicate that a child had been born at sea. Yet on the last page of the entire ship's manifest, a passenger was added:

> Trimigliozzi, Albano (born at sea) 24th January 1913, Father & Mother manifested on page 7, lines 4 & 5, final destination: Norwich, Conn.

Births, deaths, and marriages occurring during the voyage and discovered stowaways likely will be recorded on the last page of the entire manifest, but they may also be listed at the bottom of a page that has a spare line. Your only clue that something is unusual about a passenger may be a cryptic notation that the ship's purser made next to the original entry of the passenger. If you see marks you can't decipher, always check the last page of the manifest for that ship, as well as the supplemental pages that follow, known as the Record of Detained Aliens and the Record of Aliens Held for Special Inquiry (see pages 23-24).

Stowaways

Stowaways, assuming they were discovered, will be recorded either on the final page of the manifest or on an empty line on one of the other pages. Usually a notation by the person's name records him as a "stowaway," and he was detained at Ellis Island and held for the Board of Special Inquiry, with the possibility of deportation looming. If the stowaway was discovered during the voyage, he might be put to work as a crew member to work off the fare of his passage, so also check the list of crew members. If your ancestor was a stowaway, he should still be included in both microfilmed indexes and online database indexes.

Lines and Numbers

You may find lines drawn through some of the passengers' names on the list where you found your ancestor. These are people who purchased tickets—the manifest information was compiled at the time people bought their tickets—but for whatever reason, they never boarded the ship. But also note that sometimes a name was lined out but that person was actually onboard and may appear on another page of the passenger list. An immigrant may have been recorded with the steerage passengers when actually traveling second class, so the name was crossed out and moved to the correct page.

U.S. immigration officials were fond of using abbreviations. If you see "S.I." by your ancestor's name, that means he was held for the Board of Special Inquiry. You might also see stamped next to your ancestor's name "admitted" or "deported." Either one means you should go to the end of the manifest and check the pages for detained aliens and the Board of Special Inquiry, which will give you more information on that passenger.

A must-read article for interpreting numbers and annotations on your ancestor's passenger arrival list is Marian L. Smith, "Interpreting U.S. Immigration Manifest Annotations," *Avotaynu: The International Review of Jewish Genealogy* XII (Spring 1996): 10-13. This article is also online as "Manifest Markings: A Guide to Interpreting Passenger List Annotations" at <www.jewishgen.org/infofiles/manifests>.

For More Info

Record of Detained Aliens

Beginning about 1903, the passenger arrival lists began to include a supplemental section for those passengers who were detained for a variety of reasons. Many immigrants were detained for short periods of time at the port of arrival until relatives came to claim them; this was particularly true of unescorted women arrivals, whether or not they were accompanied by children.

These lists of detainees, or Record of Detained Aliens, that have survived were microfilmed with their corresponding passenger lists at the end of the manifest. The Record of Detained Aliens contains the name of each detainee, the cause for the detention, and the date and time of discharge (see Figure

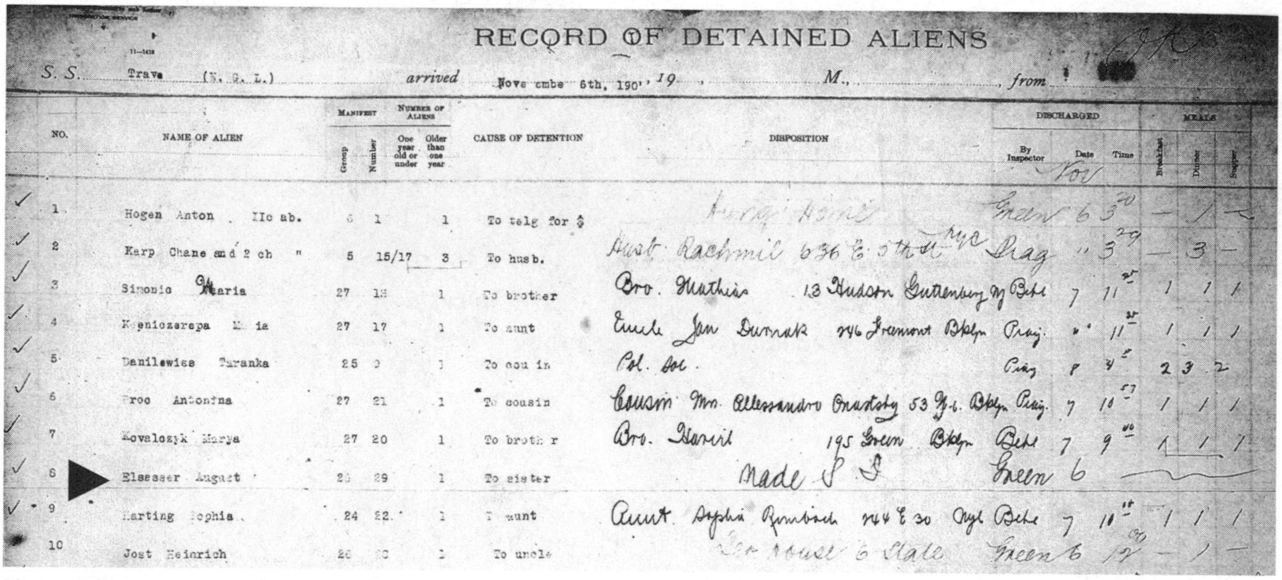

Figure 2-2
Stowaway August Elsasser was listed on the passenger list for the *Trave*, sailing from Bremen, Germany, on 26 October 1907, and arriving at the Port of New York on 6 November 1907. He was detained on Ellis Island (line 8). NARA microfilm T715, roll 1034, volume 2281.

2-2 above). You'll also find recorded the number of meals the detainee was fed during detention. If the émigré was deported before being released from Ellis Island, these records stated the reason, the date deported, and the name of the ship the deportee returned on. Once again, you might find abbreviations under the column that gives the cause of the detention. "L.P.C." meant "likely public charge" (or someone who would be destitute and needing public assistance), and "L.C.D." meant "loathsome contagious disease." These were often the two main causes for deportation. (See chapter eight for information on the medical exams at Ellis Island.)

Always check subsequent passenger lists and indexes for aliens who were deported, as they may have reentered the country at a future date when they were able to pass inspection. Another common way for deported aliens to reimmigrate was to save enough money and reenter as a first- or second-class passenger, who underwent less stringent exams aboard ship and did not have to process through Ellis Island.

Record of Detained Aliens Held for Special Inquiry

Following the Record of Detained Aliens will be a page or pages of the Record of Aliens Held for Special Inquiry (see Figure 2-3 on page 25). On this form, the cause of the detention or rejection was noted, as were actions taken by the Board of Special Inquiry, the dates of hearings, the number of meals the émigré ate during detention, and, if deported, the date and name of the vessel on which the person returned to his native land. If the rejected immigrant was waiting for someone, the form will also include the name and address of

RECORD OF ALIENS HELD FOR SPECIAL INQUIRY.

S. S. TRAVE (N. G. L.) arrived Nov. 6, 1907. , 190 , M., , from

Index No.	No.	Names	Manifest Group	Manifest No.	No. Persons	Cause of Detention	Inspector	Departmental and Executive Orders
24m	1	Elsasser, August	28	29	1	L. P. C. Green STOWAWAY; G.I. by	Leon'd	HOLD ON APPEAL
20f	2	Bartol, Ljuba, niece & nep.	3	13/5	3	Acc. alien & under 16	Rey'ds	
11f		Srakucic, Maria & bro.				" & under 16	"	
21m	3	Aranczik, Schelim	6	17	1	L. P. C.	Eager	
17f	4	Haussmann, Clara & cous.	7	28/9	2	"	Mann	
46m	5	Moldovan, Janos	23	20	1	" Dr. Memo.	Snider	
46m	6	Vinn, Bogoja	1	25	1	"	Stuck'r	
15m	7	Lowenbraum, Jakob	6	18	1	"	Eager	

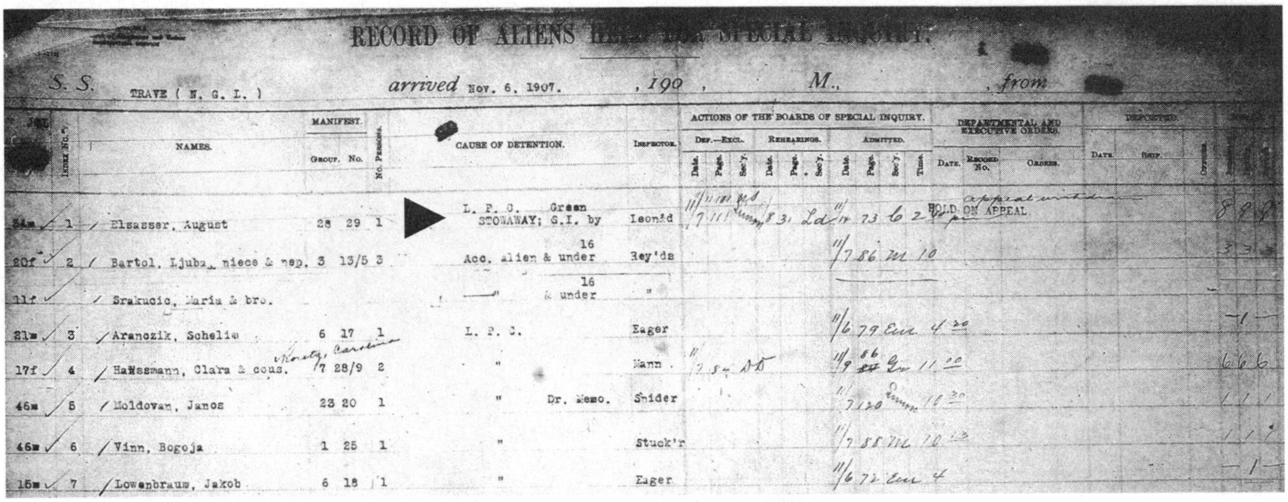

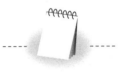

Figure 2-3
Not surprisingly, stowaway August Elsasser was held for the Board for Special Inquiry on Ellis Island. While he was detained, he ate eight breakfasts, nine dinners (lunch), and eight suppers. Evidently, he was not deported. NARA microfilm T715, roll 1034, volume 2281.

the American contact (see Deportations, Exclusions, and Quota Laws below.) **Marian L. Smith gives an excellent case study of an immigrant and his family who were held for the Special Inquiry, showing the documents that were created and explaining each step of the process in her article "Manifest Markings: Record of Aliens Held for Special Inquiry" at <www.jewishgen.org/infofiles/manifests/bsi>.**

Notes

DEPORTATIONS, EXCLUSIONS, AND QUOTA LAWS

In 1891, the federal government took control of national immigration policy and enacted laws governing the deportation of aliens. A few earlier acts excluded or limited the number of aliens allowed to enter and reside in the United States, and subsequent acts on the matter followed. New aliens deemed to be members of one of the excluded classes (see "Chronology of American Immigration Policy, 1875–1960" on page 26 for excluded classes) were briefly detained at the port until their case was decided, then sent back to the country of origin on the next returning ship of the same line; that is, they were barred from entry. Other aliens were admitted but were later charged with violation of one or another immigration law; if the charges were proved to the satisfaction of an examining board, they were deported.

Once an immigrant was admitted, the statute of limitations varied for discovery of a prior transgression or commitment of a new one, depending on the legislative act then in effect. Beginning in 1891, deportation was limited to within one year after the immigrant had been admitted. An act of 1917, however, stated that "at any time within five years of entry, any alien who at the time of entry was a member of one or more of the classes excluded by law [or] any alien who shall be found in the United States in violation of this

CHRONOLOGY OF AMERICAN IMMIGRATION POLICY, 1875–1960

1875   excluded criminals and women "brought for lewd and immoral purposes"

1882   excluded lunatics, idiots, convicts, or those likely to become a public charge; Chinese Exclusion Act; fifty-cent head tax paid by transportation company

1885   excluded contract laborers

1891   excluded paupers, offenders of "moral turpitude," polygamists, those infected with a "loathsome" or contagious disease

1894   head tax increased to $1

1903   excluded anarchists, prostitutes and their procurers, epileptics, insane persons, professional beggars; head tax increased to $2

1907   excluded the "feebleminded," children under sixteen traveling alone, anyone with a physical or mental handicap that might hinder ability to earn a living; Gentlemen's Agreement excluding Japanese laborers; head tax increased to $4 (skilled workers and whole families exempted from this tax)

1917   literacy requirement; exclusion of persons coming from Asia and the Pacific Islands; head tax increased to $8; made it a misdemeanor to bring in or harbor aliens not duly admitted by immigration officers; Mexican workers effectively restricted by head tax, literacy test, and limit of six-month stay for contracted employees

1921   first quota law (temporary), annual admission of certain ethnic groups based on a percentage of those nationalities in the 1910 census

1924   National Origins Act (second quota law), annual admission of certain ethnic groups based on 2 percent of those nationalities in the 1890 census, until 1927 when it would change to a ratio using the 1920 census; exempted Western Hemisphere countries from quotas; émigrés also needed a visa from U.S. embassy in country of origin before leaving

1929   penalties and restrictions on the return of previously deported aliens

1943   Chinese Exclusion Act was repealed; nationality law changed to allow Chinese to become citizens; authorized and financed "bracero" program to bring temporary Mexican farm workers to the United States

1945   exempted war brides of GIs from quotas

1946	facilitated admission of alien fiancés and fiancées pending marriage to U.S. military service personnel, with visiting time extended in 1947
1947	relaxed quotas and other restrictions of displaced persons from World War II, particularly favoring Polish, Czechoslovakian, Hungarian, Romanian, and Yugoslavian immigrants
1948	made it a felony to bring in or harbor aliens not duly admitted by immigration officers
1950	additional categories and extensions for displaced persons and war orphans; excluded "subversives" with any communist associations
1951	authorized Migratory Labor Agreement to continue "bracero" program importing Mexican farm labor for ten years
1952	revised quotas; removed racial barriers to naturalization; increased family preferences; excluded more classes such as subversives, lepers, drug addicts, and dealers; abolished head tax but increased various fees
1953	provided nonquota visas for refugees from Germany, Austria, and Italy; admitted children adopted by citizens serving abroad
1954	strengthened laws to deport communists; admitted sheepherders
1957	permitted enlistment of aliens to U.S. Army
1958	permitted emergency admission of Hungarian refugees
1959	extended access for orphans to be adopted; revised laws to allow entry for family members with tuberculosis
1960	expanded refugee access; excluded convicted users of marijuana

Source: E.P. Hutchinson, *Legislative History of American Immigration Policy, 1798–1965* (Philadelphia: University of Pennsylvania Press, 1981); Nicolas Kanellos with Cristelia Pérez, *Chronology of Hispanic-American History: From Pre-Columbian Times to the Present* (New York: Gale Research, 1995).

act . . . shall, upon warrant of the Attorney General, be taken into custody and deported." Another act the following year amended this to remove the five-year limitation. From 1892 to 1930, nearly 135,000 immigrants were deported. If you lose track of an immigrant or if a family story tells of a relative returning to the homeland, it may be because he or she was deported.

An alien who was barred or deported could return to America once the reason the entry was denied was corrected. So, for example, if an alien had a contagious disease (such as tuberculosis or trachoma), was sent back to the homeland, sought medical care, and became disease free, he could return again. Some saved enough money to travel in first- or second-class when they reemigrated, where the onboard inspections were not as strict as those for steerage or third-class passengers.

Existing records for barring or deporting aliens vary according to the situation.

- In open-and-shut cases involving barred aliens (prior to 1903), no special records were created. Only a notation was made on the original passenger list next to that person's name. By 1903, the name was added to a new list, called the Record of Aliens Held for Special Inquiry, created at the inspection station. These appendixes (when extant) are included in the microfilm publication of the various ship rolls, and each appears following the passenger list to which it pertains.

- Whether a Board of Special Inquiry admitted or deported an immigrant, the best information you may find is in the Record of Aliens Held for Special Inquiry. The appeals records are not as useful as you might think. Surviving records of appeals to the Board of Special Inquiry decision, which are in the custody of the National Archives in Washington, D.C., are extremely difficult to use because no finding aid or name index exists for these more than 8,000 boxes of records.

- For an alien already in the United States who was admitted but later threatened with deportation after identification as a member of an excluded class, a file was created. The Immigration and Naturalization Service (now the U.S. Citizenship and Immigration Services) pursued the case within administrative (as opposed to criminal) proceedings. Once again, these files are among the thousands of boxes of unindexed records. If you find among family papers a reference or file number for such a case, your hope of gaining access to the records would be slightly better.

An informative publication offered for free online by the U.S. Citizenship and Immigration Services (USCIS) is *An Immigrant Nation: United States Regulation of Immigration, 1798–1991* <http://uscis.gov/graphics/aboutus/history/cover.htm>. The USCIS Historical Reference Library <http://uscis.gov/graphics/aboutus/history/library.htm>, located on the first floor of the Chester Arthur Building, at 425 I Street, Northwest, Washington, D.C. 20536, phone (202) 514-2837, offers research assistance but does not have or release any records.

Now that you have an overview of passenger arrival lists and what kinds of information about your ancestors you can learn from them, let's get going and find your ancestor on a list.

CHAPTER 3

Using the Ellis Island Database

L aunched in April 2001, the Ellis Island database (EIDB), part of the American Family Immigration History Center, had more than 2.5 billion hits in its first year of operation. As of July 2003, the site had recorded more than 4.5 billion hits. On this site, you'll find more than 22 million passengers and crew members who entered through the Port of New York between 1892 and 1924—the peak years of arrival. Supposedly, it's as easy as typing in your immigrant ancestor's name. But for many of us, it's a bit more difficult than that. Before we take a step-by-step look at using the database and some tricks you need to have up your sleeves to find your missing ancestors, let's go through a basic, simple search.

LOGGING ON: THE BASICS

When you first log onto the site at <www.ellisisland.org>, you'll see a field to type in your immigrant ancestor's name under "Search Passenger Arrival Records." If you type in a name that has an exact match in the database, you'll come to another screen that will show you a list of the matching names. If the name you're looking for isn't there, click on "Close Matches Only." Assuming you find the name of a passenger you want to view, you'll click on that name, and then you'll be asked to sign in and register. There is no charge to use the site, but you will have to enter a user name and password. Of course, make sure you write these down somewhere handy, as you'll be asked for these each time you use the site. (If you're new to the site, then click on "new to the site" to register.)

Once you sign in, you'll be taken to a screen with the immigrant's passenger record. This is a typed abstract of the information from the passenger list. You can print out this information, but it won't have the pretty border that makes it look like a certificate; to get that, you'll have to purchase it. Compare this

Important

As this book was headed into production, the Ellis Island Web site was adding more search capabilities. The Morse search engine, also discussed in this chapter, was also adding features. Check for updates at <www.familytreemagazine.com>.

information with the information you've uncovered through your research to see if you have the right person. If some of the information matches what you know about the person, but other details don't, still check the actual record. You'll likely find many transcription errors, as you'll read more about later.

From the screen with the transcribed passenger record, you have three options. One is to purchase the Passenger Record certificate you see on the screen. Second is to view the "Original Ship Manifest," which displays the actual passenger ship list (manifest). Always look at the original list, as not all the information appears on the transcript, and the transcript may contain errors. Third is "Add to Your Ellis Island File," where the information will be saved.

WALKING THROUGH

Step By Step

Let's walk through a search for someone easy to find, then we'll get to more complicated searches later in the chapter.

1. On the home page <www.ellisisland.org> type in the first name "Salvatore" and the last name "Ebetino." You can leave the other fields blank for this search, but if you have information on year of birth, enter it, along with the ancestor's gender. Now click on "Start Search."

2. Only one Salvatore Ebetino will appear in the exact matches. His residence is Terlizzio [*sic*]— it should be Terlizzi—and he arrived in 1906 at the age of thirty. Click on Salvatore's name.

3. This takes you to the passenger record (transcription) that looks like a certificate. Print this information out, so you have it for your files (if he were your ancestor, of course) and to refer to while searching on the passenger list.

4. Now click on "Original Ship Manifest." Note the line number above the image, which also appears on the passenger record you initially looked at. At this point, you can still add it to your Ellis Island file, but let's click on the little magnifying glass to make the image big enough so we can read it.

5. Scroll down to line 7. There is Salvatore Ebetino. Scroll to the right using the bottom bar on your screen to view his information across the page. For this year, 1906, passengers and their information were on just one page. Later years will have two pages of information, so you'll need to close that screen out and click on "Next" to view the next page. You won't be able to print out the manifest; if you want a copy, you'll have to purchase it (each manifest page is sold separately), or see chapter four for other ways to obtain passenger lists.

Warning

Be aware that sometimes the pages of the manifest were uploaded online in reverse order. If you pull up a page with no passenger names, click the previous and next buttons to find the correct page.

Assuming your ancestor's name was transcribed correctly into the database, finding that person is as easy as the example cited. But if the name inadvertently got mangled in the transcription, it'll take a bit more creativity to find the person. Before we get into advanced searches, let's look at how the database was compiled. (Remember, the successful researcher learns something about *how* sources were created.)

BUILDING THE EIDB

The Church of Jesus Christ of Latter-day Saints headed and supervised the project to transcribe and computerize the passenger arrival lists for the years 1892–1924. Volunteer record extractors were given batches of passenger lists—photocopies from the original lists on microfilm—to transcribe. (The original lists were destroyed in the 1950s. See Appendix A beginning on page 120.) The volunteers were instructed to transcribe only genealogically significant information from the lists, such as name, age, place of birth, and so forth. According to the pamphlet "Family Record Extraction: United States Ellis Island Passenger Records," provided to directors of the project, the only manifest pages volunteers received were:

- Crew List
- List of United States Citizens
- List or Manifest of Alien Passengers for the U.S Immigration Officer at Port of Arrival
- List or Manifest of Aliens Employed on the Vessel as Members of the Crew
- Passenger List
- Report and Manifest

They were *not* given these pages to extract:

- Affidavit of the Master
- Affidavit of the Surgeon
- Changes in Crew
- Deserting Seamen
- Record of Aliens Held for Special Inquiry
- Record of Detained Aliens
- Supplement to Manifest of Alien Passengers

The project was not meant to be a complete extraction of all the information on the passenger lists. It was meant to extract only enough details for researchers to identify their ancestors in the database.

As mentioned, volunteer extractors worked with photocopies of the lists, the quality of which may have been worse than the microfilm. They were instructed, however, to check the microfilm if they were uncertain or the information wasn't clear.

Record extractors were told that they would "encounter unfamiliar names and unusual information in the records. Therefore, extractors will need to use good judgment and common sense." Thus, they did the best they could to interpret immigrants' names and other information. An extractor unfamiliar with the German clerk's script may convolute a name you might find easy to read if you've looked at records with that type of script before. For example, Angela Vallarelli came from Terlizzi, Italy. The extractor had problems reading Terlizzi, because the clerk's *T* looked like a *C*. So the extractor wrote the place of residence as "Cer. . . ." If that happened to your ancestor's *name*, you will have problems finding her in the database.

As another example, I was looking for Michael Concannon, age twenty-five, from Ireland, who arrived in 1905. The only remotely close match in the EIDB was a Michael Concan*m*on, but age seventy-five. It was worth looking at the actual list. To me, the name was clearly Concannon on the passenger list, and the age was indeed twenty-five; the extractor, however, thought the age looked like seventy-five. The lesson to be learned here, of course, is to always look at the list yourself.

Directors of the extraction project conducted audits for errors. This consisted of randomly selecting extractions from a batch and comparing them to the microfilm. If they found more than one error, all the records in that batch were to be reviewed and corrected.

Notes

If you believe a passenger's record has transcription errors, you can report these for correction. Only obvious transcription errors will be corrected. From the page with the passenger record (the one that looks like a bordered certificate), click on the "send us your corrections" link. It will generate an e-mail for you to make corrections.

USING THE EIDB

Now that you know how the database was compiled and you've performed a simple search, let's look at an example where the search wasn't so easy. Let's begin with someone I had already found on an Ellis Island passenger list in the days before the database. Several years ago, I searched for Angelina (Vallarelli) Ebetino the old-fashioned way, using microfilmed indexes and lists (more on how to do this in chapter four). Angelina arrived on the *Verona*, which left the Port of Naples on 5 February 1910 and arrived at the Port of New York on 18 February 1910. She was born in 1877.

Starting on the home page of the Ellis Island database, I typed in the name "Angelina Ebetino," her year of birth, and her gender. The results: "No records in the archive match the name Angelina Ebetino." According to the site, the choices are to

1. widen my search by using the last name I entered with only a first initial. I tried that and still no matches for an A. Ebetino.
2. widen my search by using only the last name I entered. This search returned only one record, and it was for Salvatore Ebetino, Angelina's husband. He arrived in 1906, but Angelina and their children came in 1910.
3. search on an alternate spelling of the last name. The site suggested many alternate spellings, in fact, too numerous to check.

SITE UPDATES

For those family history enthusiasts just beginning to embark on their journey of discovery, it's amazing to think of the tools that are now readily available around the clock and worldwide. In less than a decade, the centuries-old practice of researching and recording one's family history has been transformed by advances in technology. Chief among these advances is a large group of interconnected computers we have come to know as the Internet.

As recent as the mid-1990s, the majority of genealogy research was being done "the old fashioned way"—trips or letter-writing campaigns to town halls, cemeteries, libraries, and other archives containing priceless old documents with clues to an earlier generation. The copy machine and microfilm reader were the prevailing technology and an index, whether handwritten or typed, was a welcome resource that saved a great deal of page turning and eye strain. For many avid researchers, however, the most exciting and rare find at an archive was a sign reading "Open Evenings and Weekends."

The Internet quickly changed the profile of genealogical research. Simply put, the Internet made information available more often and for more researchers than at any time in history. If there was any doubt about the growing popularity of the Internet as a tool for genealogy, it disappeared on 17 April 2001. That was the day Ellis Island opened its virtual doors at <www.ellisisland.org> and received an unprecedented amount of online traffic, making it one of the most notable site launches in Internet history.

For many Americans, the passenger records documenting their ancestor's arrival through Ellis Island are among the most sought after of any historical document. Finding an ancestor's name listed among the millions of records is a thrilling and uniquely emotional experience. The Statue of Liberty–Ellis Island Foundation, through its Web site and American Family Immigration History Center® at the Ellis Island Immigration Museum, has brought this thrill and emotion to an audience much wider than ever before possible.

Throughout 2004, the Foundation studied the market and visitor feedback regarding their free Web-based service. It seemed that the growing set of online search tools on the Internet created a new set of expectations. In this age of instant gratification, many visitors expected to find their ancestor on the first search. In an effort to improve the service for both the novice and advanced researcher, the Foundation launched a number of site improvements beginning in July 2004 and continues to work on additional features as this book heads to the printer. Even seasoned researchers are reminded to visit the Web site often to keep up-to-date with changes as they are released.

Continued on next page

Highlights of the Web site improvements include the following:

1. Introduction of an "Approximate Year of Birth" field. In cases where a researcher has few details of an ancestor's arrival, it's important to help narrow the number of results using a data-point that could be determined through other sources (e.g. an obituary, headstone, vital record, or other document). When used in combination with other known facts, this feature also helps isolate an individual who may have made multiple crossings, often traveling with other family members.

2. Development of Advanced Search features. The most significant set of enhancements released during late 2004 are probably the improvements to search refinements. While the online index at <www.ellisisland.org> represented substantial time savings compared with a manual search, several enhancements to the search feature were implemented that made the process more useful to researchers. To address variations in spelling, conditional operators were added to both first and last name fields, which allow the researcher to utilize a variety of search strategies to narrow or expand their search for an individual passenger.

3. Introduction of Soundex searching. Recognizing the importance of variant spellings in passenger surnames, the site launched in 2001 with an advanced technology for recognizing names that "seemed like" a possible match when no exact match was available. These phonetic equivalents were based on a customized system and continue to be helpful for many researchers. As an additional tool, the Foundation also incorporated true Soundex search capabilities and plans to extend the function to the name fields for passenger ship and town of origin. This system is widely used in genealogical research and typically results in a wider group of possible matches, which can help uncover an entry otherwise hidden by a variant spelling or transcription error.

4. Development and introduction of a Genealogy Learning Center. This new area of the site is geared toward the novice researcher and contains how to instruction, as well as a number of free charts and forms that can be downloaded and used as a starting point in the pursuit of recording your family history. All forms can be copied and distributed for free and are especially helpful in a classroom setting.

5. Another fun addition to the Web site is the Famous Arrivals section. While some of the passengers processed at Ellis Island had already achieved fame prior to their arrival (e.g. Harry Houdini, Albert Einstein, President Theodore Roosevelt), others became famous as they or their descendants pursued the American dream. As you look through the list of famous arrivals, consider your ancestors' brush with greatness as they headed toward New York harbor.

6. Commemorative Passenger Records. The Foundation now offers an 8½″ × 11″ archival-quality certificate imprinted with the key details for a passenger's arrival (name, last place of residence, date of arrival, ship, port of departure, age, ethnicity, gender, and marital status). This keepsake joins The American Immigrant Wall of Honor® as a popular means of commemorating the arrival of a family through Ellis Island.

As you pursue your family history—whether or not your ancestors arrived through Ellis Island—please visit <www.ellisisland.org> to browse our new features. The Foundation plans to add additional capabilities in the coming months in continued response to suggestions from many of the visitors who have enjoyed the site.

—Daniel M. Lynch

So it's not as easy as it's supposed to be, is it? Let's take a deep breath and stew on this a minute. Obviously, something is wrong. I *know* she's there. But remember from chapter one that you need to know the *original name* the immigrant went by in the homeland. I realized that one of the problems was I hadn't been searching for her under the original name she used in Italy. I'm using the name she went by once she got to America. In Italy, as in some of the other Catholic countries, such as France, women were recorded in all legal documents by their *maiden* names, not their *married* names. Let's try her maiden name of Angelina Vallarelli. Nope. Still didn't get a match. Now I'll broaden the search to just A. Vallarelli. Again, no matches. Now I'll try the broadest search, clicking on just Vallarelli with no first name. Aha! There she is, but recorded as *Angela* Vallarelli. The A. Vallarelli search should have worked, but it didn't. (My research in Italian records later revealed that Angela, not Angelina, was her original name.) Obviously, you must get creative when searching for an ancestor on the Ellis Island database.

Advanced Search Features

In September 2004, the EIDB added new search features to the site, with more to come. As of this writing, here are the new features, explained in detail in the online article "Advanced Search Tips" <www.ellisisland.org/genealogy/ellis_island_search_tips_advanced.asp>:

1. First name. Four advanced search options: Ignore, Is, Starts With, and Contains [a string of two or more letters].
2. Last name. Four advanced search options: Is, Starts With, Alternate Spellings, and Sounds Like.
3. Gender. The three options are Male, Female, and Any.

Tip

Make sure you read the articles "Tips for Searching Ellis Island Passenger Records" on the Ellis Island Web site. From any page, highlight "Passenger Search" in the main menu bar. From the drop-down menu, choose "Search Tips" and "Advanced Search Tips" to access these articles. Also look for "View Tips on Preparing for a Search," a link at the bottom of each article. You'll also find helpful articles under the "Genealogy" tab of the main menu bar.

4. Approximate year of birth. You can enter an exact year or range of years.
5. Approximate year of arrival. You can enter an exact year or range of years.
6. Town/village of origin. The three options are Is, Starts With, or Contains.
7. Name of passenger ship. The three options are Is, Starts With, or Contains.
8. Ethnicity. You can choose from a list of more than 170 ethnic groups.

Step By Step

Using the Advanced Search

Let's look at another example, this time using the Advanced Search. Ignacy Pajak, an eighteen-year-old Russian immigrant from Okragla, arrived in America in 1913. Going to the EIDB and using just the basic search, type in his name. Four possibilities are listed:

1. Ignacy Pajak, from Blizne, Galicia, arriving in 1912, age 32
2. Ignacy Pajak, from Fuligtowy, Galicy, arriving in 1906, age 30
3. Ignacy Pajak, from Tuliglanz, Russia, arriving in 1913, age 38
4. Ignacy Pajak, from Tuliglowy, Galicia, arriving in 1909, age 33

The only one arriving in 1913 is too old and he's from the wrong town in Russia, but we'll check his record anyway to see if this was a transcription error. It's transcribed correctly. This isn't our Ignacy.

Let's go back to the basic Search Results. No possibilities are listed under "close matches" or alternate spellings of Pajak. Now we'll try the Advanced Search. Let's enter what we know: first name "is" Ignacy; last name "is" Pajak; male; approximate year of birth, 1895, + or - 2 years; year of arrival,

Figure 3-1
Advanced Passenger Search screen on the Ellis Island Web site.

1913, exact year; name of town "is" Okragla; and ethnicity "is" Russian. But again, no exact matches.

Let's try a search with just the first letter of his first name, and for the last name, "sounds like" Pajak. All the other fields we'll leave as we had them before. Again, no exact matches and no close matches or alternate spellings are found. We'll have to get more creative.

This time we'll ignore the first name, do a "starts with" "Pa" for the last, and try "starts with" "Ok" for the town. Oops. Currently, it won't allow a search on those parameters without entering at least three letters of the last name. By typing in the first three letters of the last name, "Paj," two possibilities come up: Rozalia Pajak, age twenty, from Oklesura, and Janacj Pajsek, age eighteen, from Okrapla. Although neither name looks familiar, we'll check the actual records to see if by chance Ignacy's entry had been mistranscribed. Sure enough, Janacj Pajsek is Ignacy Pajak! When you first view the manifest the second page loads, so click on the previous one to see the passengers' names. On line 20, where Janacj is listed, there is a name that kind of looks like Janacj Pajsek, but it also looks a lot like Ignacy Pajak, and the rest of the information about him matches what we know from other sources. We've just found our guy!

Another combination that worked was entering the last name that "sounds like" Pajak and a first name that "contains" the letters "nac";—leaving off the "Ig" in Ignacy—male; approximate year of birth, 1895, + or - 2 years; year of arrival 1913; name of town "starts with" Ok; Russian.

This search produced just one possibility: that of "Janacj Pajsek." Of course, the search potential is endless with the new advanced search tools. You could spend an entire day or more trying different combinations to unlock this safe.

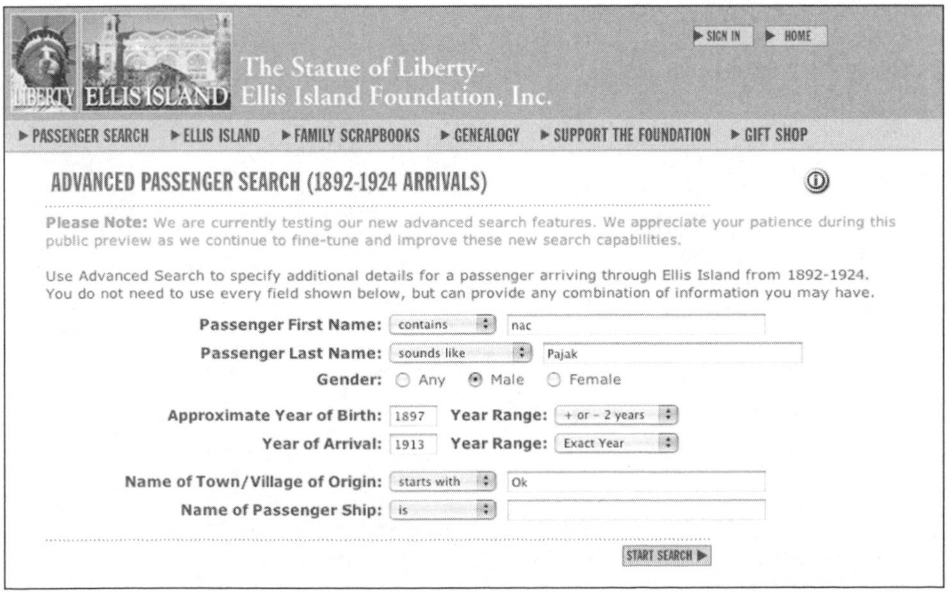

Figure 3-2
Refined advanced search, using three letters from the middle of the name "Ignacy."

THE NATURE OF ONLINE DATABASES

In just the month between the time I submitted the manuscript for this book to the publisher and when I received the copy edits back for review, new search tools went up on the Ellis Island site. This is not unusual at all. As more and more information gets uploaded and the demand increases, the search capabilities change and the site evolves. What you tried a month ago may not work now, or a new search tool will make it easier.

The point of the examples in this book isn't necessarily for you to try to duplicate the searches field-by-field, but to show you how much creativity and patience needs to go into online searching for it to be successful. By the time you read this, even more search options might be available. But don't give up! Just get creative.

OTHER SEARCH TOOLS

After the launch of the EIDB, Dr. Stephen Morse created additional search features for the EIDB, which he calls "One-Step Search Tools."

"Ellis Island Database One-Step Search Tools" is hosted by JewishGen at <www.jewishgen.org/databases/EIDB>. Here you'll find five links, but you'll want to click on the first one, "Which Ellis Island Search Form Should I Use?" which gives an overview of the various forms on the site. Although

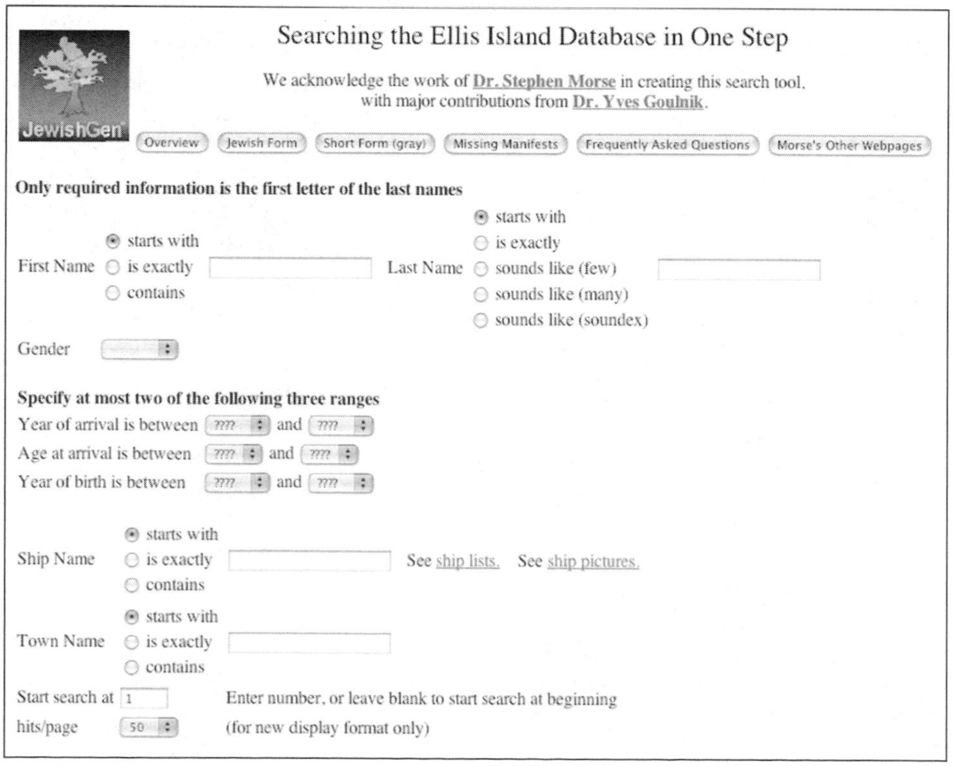

Figure 3-3
Screen capture (entire page not shown) of the JewishGen site for searching the Ellis Island Database in One Step.

the Ellis Island database was adding new search features as this book was in production, the Morse database was the only site you could use to search by town name, port, or passenger ship without first entering a passenger name. **This allows you to perform a search to find all the people who came from your ancestor's village during a given year, or you can do a search for just the ship and read the entire manifest.** But as Morse cautions, the town search capability has serious limitations, namely the town name "must be spelled (or misspelled as the case may be) exactly as it appears in the Ellis Island database for the passenger you are seeking. . . . Of course you have no way of knowing in advance exactly how it was entered." So the town-search feature is currently of limited value. For an alternate type of town-search feature, use his short form search. Before you use Morse's search forms, it's well worth your time to read all the Frequently Asked Questions under each form.

Research Tip

Searching for Ignacy Pajak

Let's start all over and pretend we haven't found Ignacy and the unfortunate mistranscription of his name. Using Ignacy Pajak, his correct name, in Morse's tools, let's see if and how we need to modify our search there. We'll begin with the white search form. Let's leave off the first name and just enter the surname, his age at arrival (eighteen), and the year 1913. We'll also add that his ethnicity is Russian, and we'll click on the button for "search (new format)." The old format takes you directly to the EIDB; the new one gives you all the links from the site: that is, you can go to the links to view the passenger record, text manifest, scanned manifest, or the ship, and it gives all the villages of origin. This search still didn't give me any possible matches. So let's get creative again. Although you could enter just the first letter of the surname with the year and age, often the site will "time out" before it gives you any matches. So let's enter just "Pa," male, age eighteen, year of arrival 1913, and check the ethnicity "Russian." This search returned 225 possibilities. Since we know that the name is not what we expect it to be, we'll look at the residence column to see if we can make a match that way. There is an entry for Janacj Pajsek from Okrapla, Russia. We know this is actually Ignacy Pajak from Okragla. He arrived on the *Lapland*, sailing from Antwerp on 14 June 1913, and arriving in New York on 22 June 1913. (See chapter four for finding Ignacy in the microfilmed Soundex.)

USING OTHER CLUES

Another technique to finding your ancestors in the EIDB or through Morse's tools is to search for relatives or friends who came with your ancestor. See how this technique became a success story for Sharon Freel Schwarz of Massapequa, New York.

Technique

My grandparents Nicholas Gladky and Anastasia Schuleiko died in an automobile accident when I was sixteen months old. When I became interested in family history, I realized I needed much more family information. I remember asking my mother for the correct spelling of Grandma's name. She told me it was spelled "Schuleiko" or "Shulejko" or "something like that." It amazed me that she wasn't sure how to spell her mother's maiden name. She explained to me that back then people weren't as concerned with how the name was spelled, since many immigrants couldn't spell anyway. The name variations of Schuleiko, Shuleiko, Shulejko, and Shulaka all "sounded" alike.

Both of my grandparents immigrated through Ellis Island in 1913. I was told they came from Poland and Russia. Finding their respective ship manifests should be easy. I had a copy of their naturalization certificates and their certificates of arrival issued by the Immigration and Naturalization Service. I wrote to the National Archives and received the manifest for my grandfather, but for my grandmother I received the dreaded reply: "The record you requested was not found." I thought, "How could that be?" I had "proof" of her arrival. I looked again at her certificate of arrival, and I hadn't misread it:

Name: Anastasia Shuleiko, now Anastasia Gladky
Port of Entry: New York
Date: July 27, 1913
Manner of Arrival: *SS Kaiser Franz Joseph I*

If I had this record, then why couldn't NARA find her on their ship passenger arrival records? I assumed that they hadn't done a thorough search, and I'd have to write to them again.

But then the Ellis Island database appeared online, so I decided it was time to find my grandmother myself. I typed her name into the fields and was surprised that it didn't find her. I tried Schuleiko, Schulejko, Shuleiko, Shuleijko, Shulaka. I tried it in combinations with and without "Anastasia." Still no Grandma! Now I had to get creative and try another way of finding her.

Within my box of family papers, I found a typewritten paper my grandmother had made. It was a summary of the important details of her life, listing her maiden and married names, and all her addresses since entering the United States. She gave her nationality as Russian, but her place of birth as Poland. This paper, too, listed her immigration as 27 July 1913 on the *SS Kaiser Franz Joseph I*, as Anastasia Shuleiko. She was coming to Jersey City, New Jersey, to join her cousin Bronislaw Lebiedziewicz, and she was accompanied on the voyage by Amelia Rajko. I read that twice. Another clue!

I ran back to my computer and tried the Ellis Island database again, this time looking for Amelia Rajko. But still my search came up empty. Next I tried typing in just the surname Rajko. Again, no Amelia. I scanned through the forty-eight exact matches for Rajko, and finally one caught my eye. Even though there was no Amelia, there *was* an Emilia Rajko, who had also immigrated to the United States in 1913—the same year as Grandma. I clicked on the link for Emilia Rajko, and it revealed that she had arrived on 22 July 1913 on the ship *Martha Washington*. That certainly didn't match my grandmother's information; her certificate of arrival stated she'd arrived five days later on the *Kaiser Franz Joseph I*. I was getting frustrated.

Out of complete desperation, I clicked on the "View Original Ship Manifest" button. There on line 22 was Emilia Rajko, and just above her name, on line 21, was an eighteen-year-old female named *Stasia Szulejka*. Could it be she? Was this my grandmother? I read through the rest of the information for line 21, and sure enough, Stasia Szulejka was coming to New Jersey to join her cousin Bronislaw Lebiedziewicz. I had found my grandmother at last.

The lesson I learned was to read every record you have for all clues and be creative in your search. I have since learned that in the Polish/Russian language *Sz* is pronounced *Sh* or *Sch*, which explains all the spelling variations of Schuleiko, Shulejko, Shulaka, and Szulejka. Anastasia Schuleiko, meet Stasia Szulejka!

Sharon demonstrates concisely how important relatives, friends, associates, or neighbors can be when tracking immigrant arrivals. If you're not finding your ancestor in the passenger records—whether it be electronically or on microfilm—go back to other sources, such as oral history, family papers, and censuses, and take note of other people named in those documents. People rarely migrated to another area alone. They almost always came with someone or were going to join someone in the adopted homeland. When your search for your ancestor is negative, look for those people, too.

Notice, too, that her grandmother's documents incorrectly recorded the ship name and arrival date. More research would be necessary to learn what might have happened in this situation. Both ships, the *Kaiser Franz Joseph I* and the *Martha Washington*, sailed for the Austro-American Line from the Adriatic to New York. Perhaps Anastasia had purchased a ticket on the *Kaiser Franz Joseph I*, but she was able to depart a week earlier on the *Martha*

Important

Washington. Then again, we may never know what happened. Fortunately, Schwarz kept an open mind and explored the clues she had; otherwise, she may have never found her grandmother.

MISSING MANIFESTS AND WRONG LINKS

You may get a hit on your ancestor's name in either the EIDB or on the Morse search form, but when you click on the "View Original Ship Manifest" button you may be unfortunate enough to have it take you to the wrong ship! This happened in my search for eighteen-year-old August Elsasser from Rotenburg, Germany, who stowed away on the *Trave* in 1907. After you get the passenger record on the EIDB, then click on the original manifest to view, it takes you to the ship *Kronprinzessin Cecilie*, which also arrived in 1907, but it wasn't the ship I needed.

Fortunately, you can search by ship using the link on the JewishGen site under "Missing Manifests," or go directly to <www.stevemorse.org/ellis/boat .html>. Here, I typed in the name of the ship, *Trave*, and year of arrival. It gave me a list of six times when the *Trave* arrived at New York that year, along with the NARA microfilm series T715, roll numbers, volumes, and the date. The one I needed for August Elsasser was 6 November 1907, roll 1034, volume 2281. When I clicked on that ship's arrival, it took me to the first frame of volume 2280, which contained the passenger lists for the *Kronprinzessin Cecilie*. I tried everything I could think of to get to the next volume that would have the *Trave* on it, but nothing I did would bring up that roll.

In one of the FAQs, Morse told of a user who searched for his relative and was taken to the manifest for the wrong ship. He noted the name of the passenger who was on the line that his relative was supposed to be on. Then he searched for that passenger and found his relative. This may have worked for this user, but it sure didn't work for me. The passenger who came up for August Elsasser's page was Otto Schmidt. When I searched for Otto, it took me to the page of the *Kronprinzessin Cecilie* where Otto was listed.

At a loss of what to do next, I contacted Morse, and he directed me to FAQ #415 under the white form page: "Is there an easy way to go directly to the roll and frame for a particular ship arrival?" "Yes," writes Morse, "Go to my Ship Lists page and enter the ship name and a range of dates. This gives you a list of arrivals. You click on the one you want and that gets you to the correct microfilm roll on my missing-manifest form. Often this will get you right to the first frame for the ship that you want. But sometimes this will get you to the first frame on the roll instead. That's because I have not yet completed tabulating the ship details for all the rolls. This is part of an ongoing project and if you would like to help out so that others can find their ships easier, click here. To see a list of which rolls are fully tabulated and which still need to be worked on, click here." While frustrating, we have to keep in mind all the volunteer work and time that goes into creating a project like this, and it's not all complete when we need it.

So how can I get a copy of that passenger list for the *Trave* with August Elsasser on it? The old-fashioned way: searching the microfilm.

USING MICROFILM VS. COMPUTERIZED IMAGES

Anyone who has used both microfilm and computerized images knows that it is far quicker to crank through a roll of microfilm than it is to download computer images of passenger lists, especially if you're using a dial-up modem rather than a high-speed Internet connection. Sometimes the lists span two pages, so it takes several minutes to view your ancestor's full list. And some of the pages, for whatever reason, were uploaded out of order. So you might land on the second page of information and have to click on the previous page. The images of pages that do not include passenger information were also digitized, making it quite time-consuming if you wanted to view the whole ship's list or to go to the end of the list to check for detained aliens and those held for the Board of Special Inquiry. On the other hand, the computerized images are digitally enhanced, and oftentimes are much easier to read than the microfilm. Certainly nothing's wrong with using a combination of both microfilmed and computerized passenger lists, so let's look now at how to use the microfilm and its indexes.

CHAPTER 4

Back to Microfilm Basics

Microfilm Source

A lthough the launch of the Ellis Island database and Morse's search forms have revolutionized the ease and convenience with which you can find your ancestors on passenger lists, as we saw in chapter three, if you aren't finding your ancestor, then all the fancy bells and whistles of Internet searching won't matter. **Fortunately, you have another way to discover your ancestors on passenger lists, and that's by doing it the way genealogists have done it for decades: using microfilms of passenger lists and indexes.**

INDEXES TO PASSENGER ARRIVAL LISTS

As mentioned in chapter one, to identify an immigrant in any index or passenger list, you must have enough information (e.g., original name, age or birth date, approximate date of arrival) from other sources to find and properly identify the right immigrant. A foreign name that seems unique in America may be as common as John Smith in the homeland. Knowing approximately how old the immigrant was upon arrival will help you eliminate others by the same name in the index. Knowing approximately when your ancestor arrived helps you narrow your search. Knowing the town of origin or names of relatives or neighbors in America with whom your ancestor may have traveled will help you eliminate other passengers of the same name. Keep in mind, also, that names were often recorded as they were heard. Many emigrants were illiterate and did not know how to spell their names, even if asked. Shipping company clerks often recorded the name as they heard it, so check for spelling variations.

For the Port of New York, microfilmed indexes cover the years 1820–1846, 1897–1902, 1902–1943, and 1944–1948. (Online indexes cover 1851–1891 on Ancestry.com and 1892–1924 on EllisIsland.org.) You can view microfilmed indexes for the Port of New York at the National Archives in Washington, D.C., at NARA's Northeast Region facility in New York City, at the Family History Library in Salt Lake City, Utah, and through one of its worldwide Family History Centers.

The microfilmed indexes to the Port of New York are on 3″ × 5″ cards. Some of these card indexes will be arranged alphabetically; others use the Soundex code (see "Soundex Coding" on page 47). The alphabetical ones may not be in strict alphabetical order, however, or may be misfiled. Here is how they are supposed to be arranged for the Port of New York:

1897–1902	Alphabetically by surname, then by given name
1902–1943	Surnames A-D, arranged by Soundex code, then alphabetically by the first letter or first two letters of the given name, then by date of arrival (or volume number when date is not given) Surnames D-Z, arranged by Soundex code, then alphabetically by given name, followed by those whose age was not given (for the years 1903–1910), then by age at arrival

If you don't find your ancestor, check for him or her by initials instead of a full given name (Otto Schmidt vs. O. Schmidt), and check for variant spellings. Women belonging to some ethnic groups (typically Italian and French) will likely be indexed and recorded under their maiden names, not their married surnames. If you don't know your female ancestor's maiden name, but she traveled with either her husband or her children, look for them in the index. The children should be recorded under their father's surname.

A word of caution: Once you have Soundexed the surname and put the appropriate roll of microfilm on the reader, the index cards should be ar-

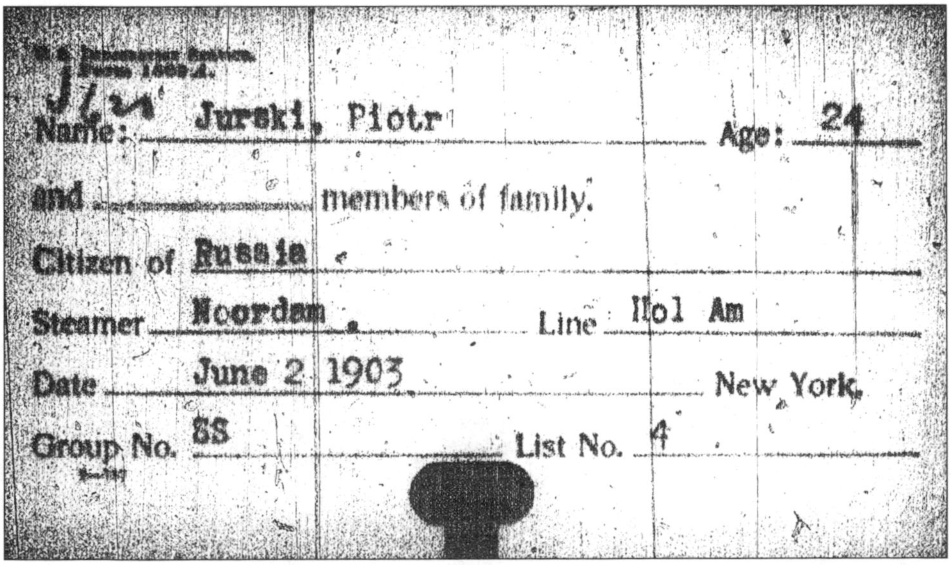
J/24
Name: Jureki, Piotr Age: 24
and ____ members of family.
Citizen of Russia
Steamer Noordam Line Hol Am
Date June 2 1903 New York
Group No. 88 List No. 4

Figure 4-1
Index (Soundex) to passenger lists of vessels arriving at New York, New York, 1 July 1902–31 December 1943. Copy all the information from the Soundex card and consult with the staff or the NARA publication *Immigrant and Passenger Arrivals: A Select Catalog of the National Archives Microfilm Publications*, second edition, to find the roll of microfilm you need for the passenger arrival list.

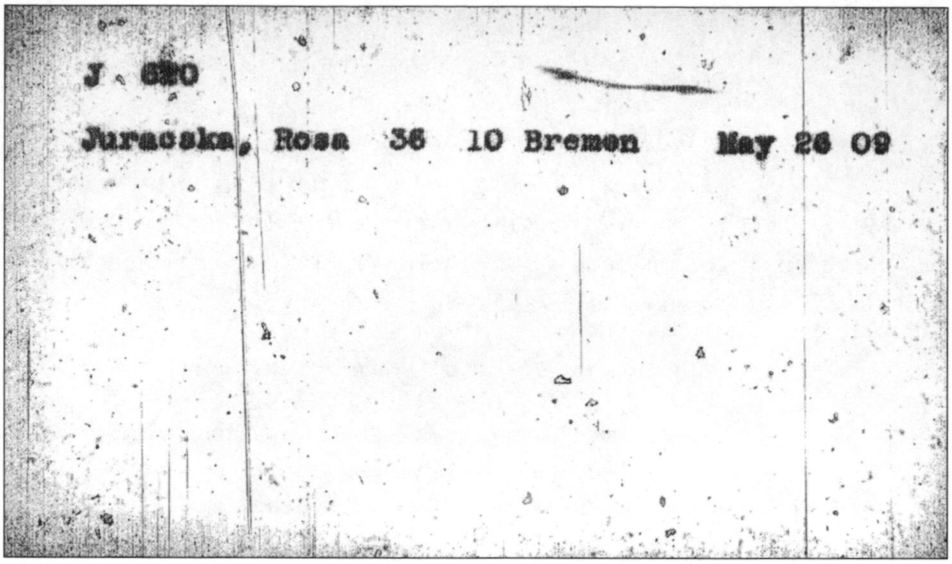

Figure 4-2
Index (Soundex) to passenger lists of vessels arriving at New York, New York, 1 July 1902–31 December 1943. Once you have the information from the card, consult with the staff or the NARA publication *Immigrant and Passenger Arrivals: A Select Catalog of the National Archives Microfilm Publications*, second edition, to find the roll of microfilm you need for the passenger arrival list.

Warning

ranged alphabetically by the person's *first name*. **Some rolls have cards arranged by year of arrival, however, then alphabetically by the first name.** To make sure you don't miss your ancestor, scan the cards after you find the Soundex code on the microfilm to make sure which arrangement that roll of film is using.

The index cards will have different formats, depending on the arrival year. Some of the cards are a form with all the information written out, giving passenger's name, age, group number, list number, sex, citizenship, steamer, line, date, and port. But other cards may baffle you. Identifying the name is no problem, but what are all those other numbers? The Soundex code number is always in the upper left corner.

Below is a guide to the other information on the cards during different years, which pertains to the cards for the Port of New York. (Other ports may have their own irregularities.)

December 1903–June 1910	name, group number, list number, vessel, date of arrival
July 1910–1937	name, age/sex, list number, group number, volume number
1937–June 1942	*top line after Soundex code:* month/year; *center line:* name, age/sex, list number, group number, volume number; *bottom line:* vessel
July 1942–December 1943	*top line:* Soundex code, vessel or plane, date; *center line:* name, age/sex, list number, group number, volume number

Copy all the information from the index card. The microfilm rolls for the

SOUNDEX CODING

The Soundex indexing system, invented by Robert C. Russell in 1918, is based on the way a name sounds rather than how it is spelled, so that names with similar sounds will be coded together. This indexing system is important for you to learn, since many federal records, such as passenger arrival lists, use the Soundex. All surnames are coded using the first letter of the surname, followed by a three-digit number, like this one for Carmack: C652. Before going step-by-step through how this works, here is how the letters are coded with numbers:

The Number	Represents the following letters:
1	B P F V
2	C S K G J Q X Z
3	D T
4	L
5	M N
6	R

The letters *A, E, I, O, U, W, Y,* and *H* are disregarded. And the first letter of a surname is not coded; it is used as the first part of the code. You code only the first three consonants in a name.

Let's say that I am searching for the surname Gordon. In order to Soundex it, I would start with the first letter of the surname, *G*, which is not assigned a numeral. Then I would cross out all the vowels, *w, y,* and *h*:

G e r d o n

Now I am left with the consonants *r, d,* and *n,* which I will convert to numerals. *R* becomes a 6, *d* becomes a 3, and *n* becomes a 5; so the Soundex code for Gordon is G635. Let's try another example: Vallarelli. New rules will apply to this name, but let's begin with the basics. The first letter is not coded, so the Soundex will begin with the letter *V*. Now we cross out all the vowels, *w, y,* and *h*.

V a l l a r e l l i

We're left with *l, l, r, l, l*. Now here's the next new rule: if you have double consonants or two or more of the same consonants together after crossing out the vowels, only one of them will be coded. So we are now going to cross out two of the *l*s.

V a l l a r e l l i

Now we're left with just *l, r, l*. So the Soundex code for Vallarelli is V464.

Continued on next page

More new rules: If you have more than three consonants left, code only the first three and ignore the rest. If you have fewer than three consonants, add zeros. For example, Lee would be coded L000, since it has only vowels and no consonants.

If the surname has a prefix, like in DeBartolo, code it both with the prefix (D163) and without it (B634), since the Soundex is not consistent as to whether the indexer coded it with or without the prefix.

At first, this system seems difficult and confusing, but remember that wherever you go to view the census and use the Soundex system, an attendant or volunteer will be available to help you code your surnames. Or, you can visit Roots-Web.com <http://resources.rootsweb.com/cgi-bin/soundexconverter>, type in your surname, and it will code it for you.

passenger lists will be cataloged differently in different repositories, so check with the librarian or archivist to find the roll with the date you need from the information on the index. Regardless of how the films are cataloged, however, they are all publications of the National Archives and the arrival lists are microfilmed in roughly chronological order, although some lists may be out of sequence.

After putting the roll on the microfilm reader, you will find that typically two to three "volumes" of manifests are filmed on one roll. A title sheet precedes each volume, giving you the volume number, the dates of arrival, the names of the steamships in the order they have been microfilmed, the ports of departure, and how many sheets each manifest contains.

Once you find the ship's list, you will use the other information from the index card to find the exact page. The "list number" on the index card refers to the line number on the manifest, running down the left side of the sheet. The group number is the tricky one. You will probably see several numbers on each passenger list page: stamped numbers, numbers handwritten in grease pencil, numbers on the bottom of the page, and numbers at the top. Once again, the placement of the group number varied, depending on the year. Here is the breakdown for the Port of New York:

Location of Group Number on the Passenger List

1897–1902	usually top right corner
1902–1908	usually grease pencil or stamped numbers at top left
1908–1943	usually stamped numbers at bottom left

Before June 1910 the index gives the date of arrival; after that date, it gives the volume number. To match the volume number with the date, you will need to complete an extra step. Consult the finding aid *Immigrant and Passenger*

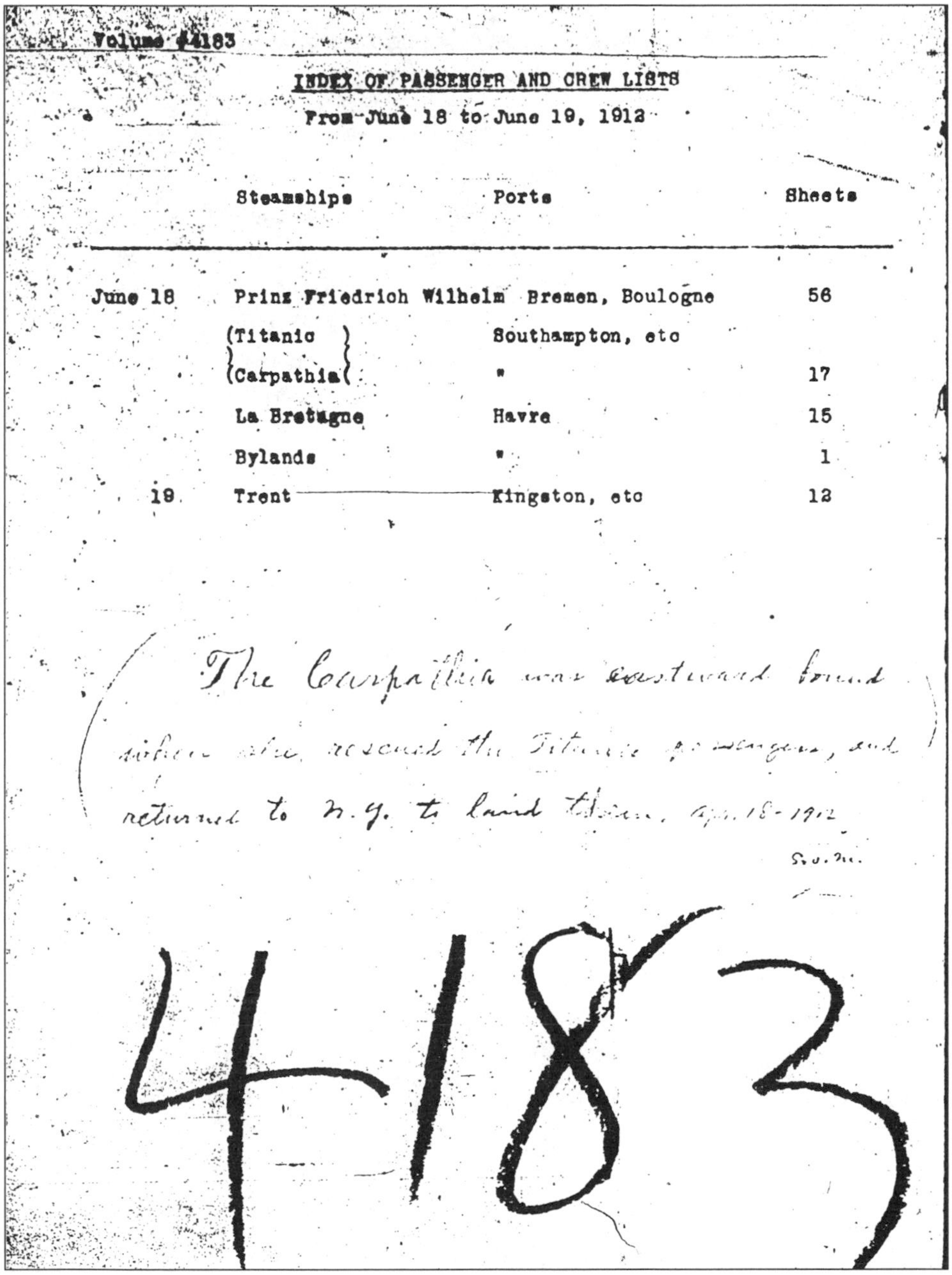
Volume 4183

INDEX OF PASSENGER AND CREW LISTS
From June 18 to June 19, 1912

	Steamships	Ports	Sheets
June 18	Prinz Friedrich Wilhelm	Bremen, Boulogne	56
	(Titanic	Southampton, etc	
	(Carpathia	"	17
	La Bretagne	Havre	15
	Bylands	"	1
19	Trent	Kingston, etc	12

The Carpathia was eastward bound when she rescued the Titanic passengers, and returned to N.Y. to land them. Apr. 18-1912

4183

Figure 4-3
Usually two or three "volumes" of lists are on each roll of microfilm. The title sheet to each volume precedes the lists it covers. Volume 4183 of NARA microfilm T715, roll 1883, contains the arrival list, among others, for the *Titanic.* The notation reads, "The *Carpathia* was eastward bound when she rescued the *Titanic* passengers, and return to N.Y. to land them. Apr. 18- 1912."

Arrivals: A Select Catalog of National Archives Microfilm Publications online at <www.archives.gov/publications/microfilm_catalogs/immigrant/immigrant_passenger_arrivals.html> to find the appropriate volume number, which will list the date of arrival for that volume, along with the National Archives microfilm roll number. If you are at the Family History Library in Salt Lake City, then consult the immigration finding-aid binder labeled "NYC Immigration Register, 1820–1943" (although the title page is labeled "Register of New York City Passenger Lists") at the reference tables of the United States/Canada floor. Look for the volume number, which gives you the date of arrival, followed by the library's microfilm call number.

BOOK INDEXES TO NEW YORK ARRIVALS

Another set of indexes for the Port of New York, called *Book Indexes to New York Passenger Lists, 1906–1942*, has been microfilmed by the National Archives and is also available through the Family History Library. These alphabetical book indexes were compiled by steamship companies at the same time they prepared the passenger list, so they are grouped by the shipping line, then arranged chronologically by date of arrival. The drawback, of course, is you must know the name of the ship, the date of arrival, then find the name of the shipping line, which you can find in the *Morton Allan Directory* on page 61.

If you are at a Family History Center and they don't have a printout of the New York passenger lists volumes and films, your task might be a bit more tedious. On FamilySearch.org, go to "Library," "Family History Library Catalog," then under "Place Search," type in New York City. You will be presented with a list of five burroughs and the city itself—click on the link to the city. When you get to the list of topics, click on "emigration and immigration." Then click on the link for "Index to passenger lists of vessels arriving at New York, June 16, 1897–June 30, 1902; Index (Soundex) to passenger lists of vessels arriving in New York, July 1, 1902–December 31, 1943; Passenger and crew lists of vessels arriving at New York." From there, you'll click on "View Film Notes," which will take you to more than 7,700 rolls of microfilm! To get to the volumes for June 1910 and later, at the bottom of the first page, type in 2425, and that will fast-forward you to the correct volumes. From there you keep advancing (or typing in higher page numbers) to get to the appropriate volume you need. (This is also the group of records you'll use to find the correct microfilm to order the index.)

PUTTING IT INTO PRACTICE

Step By Step

Remember Ignacy Pajak from the last chapter and all the trouble we had finding him in the database? **Let's see what happens when we look for him in the microfilmed Soundex.** Coding the surname Pajak, it falls under P220 (see "Soundex Coding" on page 47 for how to Soundex names). We'll go to that roll of film and look for Ignacy there. Several men listed are named Ignacy, and lo and behold, an Ignacy Pajak, age eighteen.

The card shows he can be found in volume 4782. Go to the finding aids for that volume—in this case the binder on the Family History Library's reference shelf labeled "NYC Immigration Register, 1820–1943"—but you could also go to the *Immigrant and Passenger Arrivals: A Select Catalog of National Archives Microfilm Publications* online or check the Family History

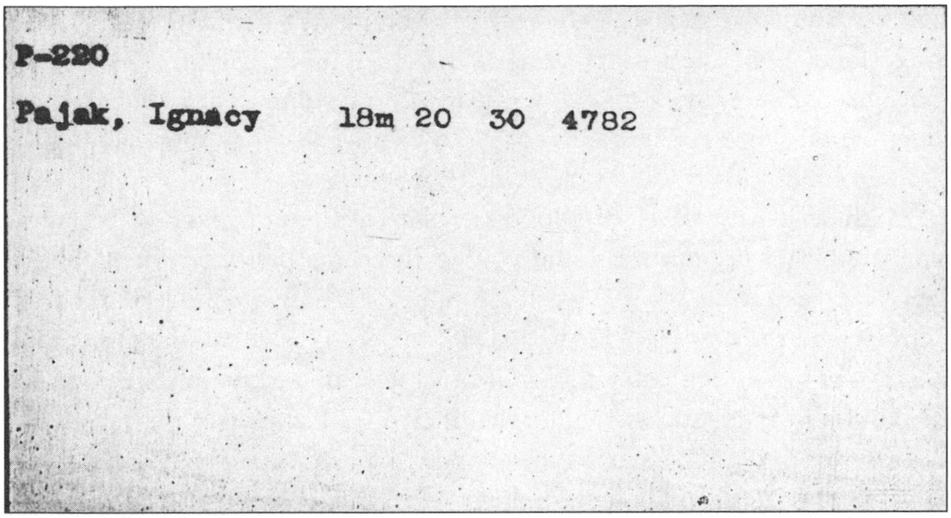

P-220

Pajak, Ignacy 18m 20 30 4782

Figure 4-4
On the Soundex card, Ignacy Pajak's name was transcribed correctly. The numbers reference his age and sex (18m), the line number on the passenger list (20), group number (30), and the volume (4782). By consulting with *Immigrant and Passenger Arrivals: A Select Catalog of the National Archives Microfilm Publications*, second edition, you'll find that this volume covers the year 1913. Index (Soundex) to passenger lists of vessels arriving at New York, New York, 1 July 1902–31 December 1943.

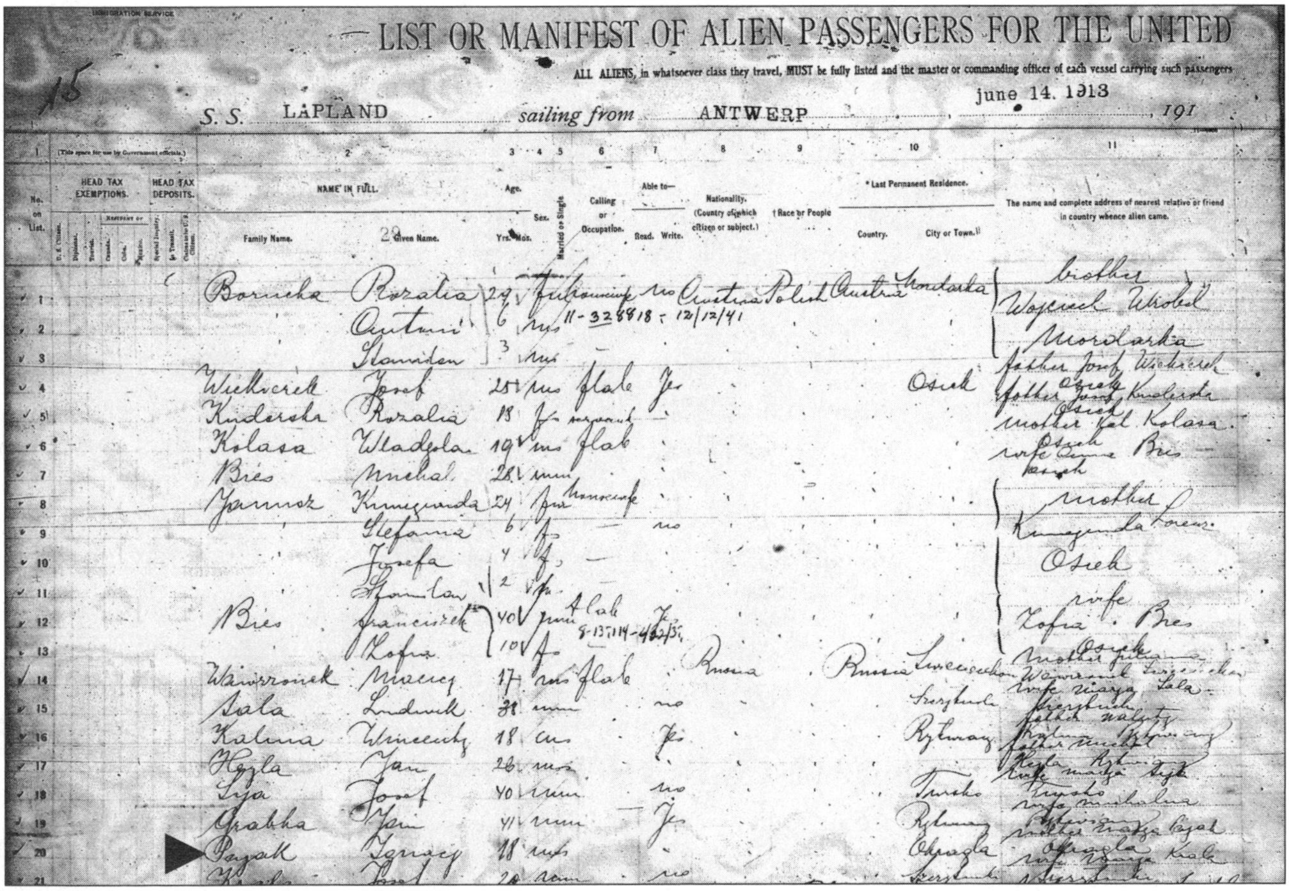

LIST OR MANIFEST OF ALIEN PASSENGERS FOR THE UNITED

ALL ALIENS, in whatsoever class they travel, MUST be fully listed and the master or commanding officer of each vessel carrying such passengers

S. S. LAPLAND sailing from ANTWERP june 14. 1913, 191

Figure 4-5
Ignacy Pajak is on line 20 of the passenger list for the *Lapland*, sailing from Antwerp on 14 June 1913, and arriving at the Port of New York, 22 [23] June 1913. The second page of this list (not shown) gives additional information on each passenger. By looking at the list, you can understand how the modern-day transcriber read the name as "Janacj Pajsek" for the Ellis Island database. NARA microfilm T715, roll 2112, volume 4782.

Library catalog as mentioned on page 50. Volume 4782 is for the arrival date of 23 June 1913. The actual finding aid recorded the arrival of 22 June 1913, but Ignacy's ship, the *Lapland*, was part of this volume. (It may have been due to arrive on the 22nd, but was a day late.) The card shows that Ignacy is in group 30, list 20, and indeed, that's where he is.

Gosh, that was a heck of a lot easier than using the database! When the spelling hasn't been misread and you hit the name perfectly, the databases are the best invention in the world. (You can see how the modern-day transcriber read the name as "Janacj Pajsek" for the Ellis Island database, can't you?) But when you can't find your ancestor, don't give up. Turn to the microfilm indexes (Soundex). Not that they're perfect either, but they can be a lot easier to use. One reason the Soundex indexes might be more accurate is those who were compiling the indexes several decades ago were more accustomed to reading handwritten documents. Today's data entry transcribers (often college-age staff) are more used to seeing items typewritten. Additionally, styles of handwriting changed over the decades, so those indexing a record closest to its creation could probably read the writing style much easier than someone today reading passenger lists of eighty or more years ago.

DAITCH-MOKOTOFF SOUNDEX SYSTEM

Randy Daitch and Gary Mokotoff created this Soundexing system when they discovered that the Russell system wasn't useful enough to accurately code many Eastern European Jewish names. Many of these names that sounded the same did not code the same, such as names like Moskowitz and Moskovitz, which use the letters *w* and *v* interchangeably. For more information and the rules governing this system, see Gary Mokotoff's "Soundexing and Genealogy" <www.avotaynu.com/soundex.html>. As this book went into publication, the Daitch-Mokotoff System was not available on the Ellis Island database search tools (discussed in chapter three), but it is part of the Morse tools <www.jewishgen.org/databases/EIDB>, which you can use to search the Ellis Island database.

FINDING ESTER AHLQUIST

Case Study

According to family stories, Ester Ahlquist came to America in 1912 through the Port of New York. Family members remember it was April of 1912 because that was the same month and year the *Titanic* sank, but Ester's ship docked after the world-famous disaster. She was from Sweden, around seventeen or eighteen when she emigrated, and she came alone, as did so many young Swedish women of her time.

The first step is to Soundex Ester's last name, Ahlquist, as A422, so I could check the index to New York passenger lists. Among the index cards were two possible matches:

> Ahlquist, Ester   17f 16 25 4085
>
> Ahlquist, Ester   17f   9 91 6633

Checking *Immigrant and Passenger Arrivals: A Select Catalog of National Archives Microfilm Publications*, volume 4085 is for ships arriving on 18 April 1912, and volume 6633 is for vessels arriving on 27 November 1920. Obviously, the first listing is the one I need (see Figure 4-6 below).

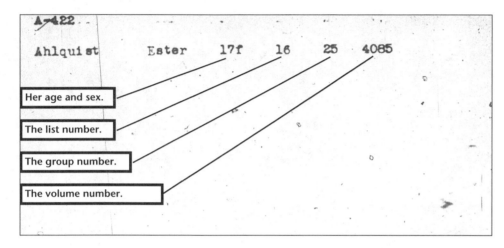

Figure 4-6
Index (Soundex) to passenger lists of vessels arriving at New York, for Ester Ahlquist's passenger arrival.

After finding the appropriate microfilm and putting it on the microfilm reader, I came to a title page showing two ships in that volume, docking at New York: *Hellig Olav* from Copenhagen and *Athinai* from Palermo, Italy. Since Ester's Swedish, the ship she came on was more than likely the ship from Copenhagen (see Figure 4-7 on page 54).

The two other numbers on the index card were 16 and 25. For the year 1912, these numbers are the list and group numbers, respectively. The list number will be the column of vertical numbers on the left side of the page; the group number is the one I need to find on the many pages of the passenger list. Also for 1912, this group number is usually going to appear as a stamped number on the bottom left of each sheet. After I find number 25, I then look at the list numbers for number 16. Sure enough, there's Ester in the third class, or steerage, compartment.

Here is what the passenger list information showed on page one of the manifest (see Figure 4-8 on page 55):

- The ship left Copenhagen on 4 April 1912 and docked at the Port of New York on 18 April 1912
- Name: Ahlquist, Ester
- Age: 17
- Sex: f[emale]

Figure 4-7
Title page for volume 4085, found on NARA microfilm T715, roll 1843. Ester no doubt came on the ship *Hellig Olav*, which departed Copenhagen, rather than the ship that left from Palermo.

Volume number may be typed or handwritten in grease pencil, or both.

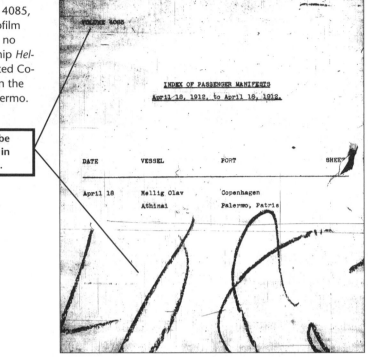

- Married or single: single
- Occupation: servant
- Able to read and write: yes
- Nationality: Sweden
- Race or People: Scandinavian [denoted by ditto marks]
- Last Permanent Residence: Country: Sweden [denoted by ditto marks], City or Town: Helleberga [Hallsberg?]
- Name and complete address of nearest relative or friend in county whence alien came: father, Y.G. Ahlquist, Moleras
- Final destination: State: NJ [New Jersey], City or Town: Princeton

Page two of the manifest (see Figure 4-9 on page 56):
- Whether having a ticket to such final destination: no
- By whom was passage paid: self
- Whether in possession of $50, and if less, how much: $30
- Whether ever in the United States, and if so, when and where: no [if she had answered yes, I would check for another passenger list]
- Whether going to join a relative or friend, and if so, what relative or friend, and his name and complete address: sister, Alina Wright, 24 Chestnut [unreadable], Princeton, NJ
- Ever in prison, almshouse: no
- Whether a polygamist: no
- Whether an anarchist: no

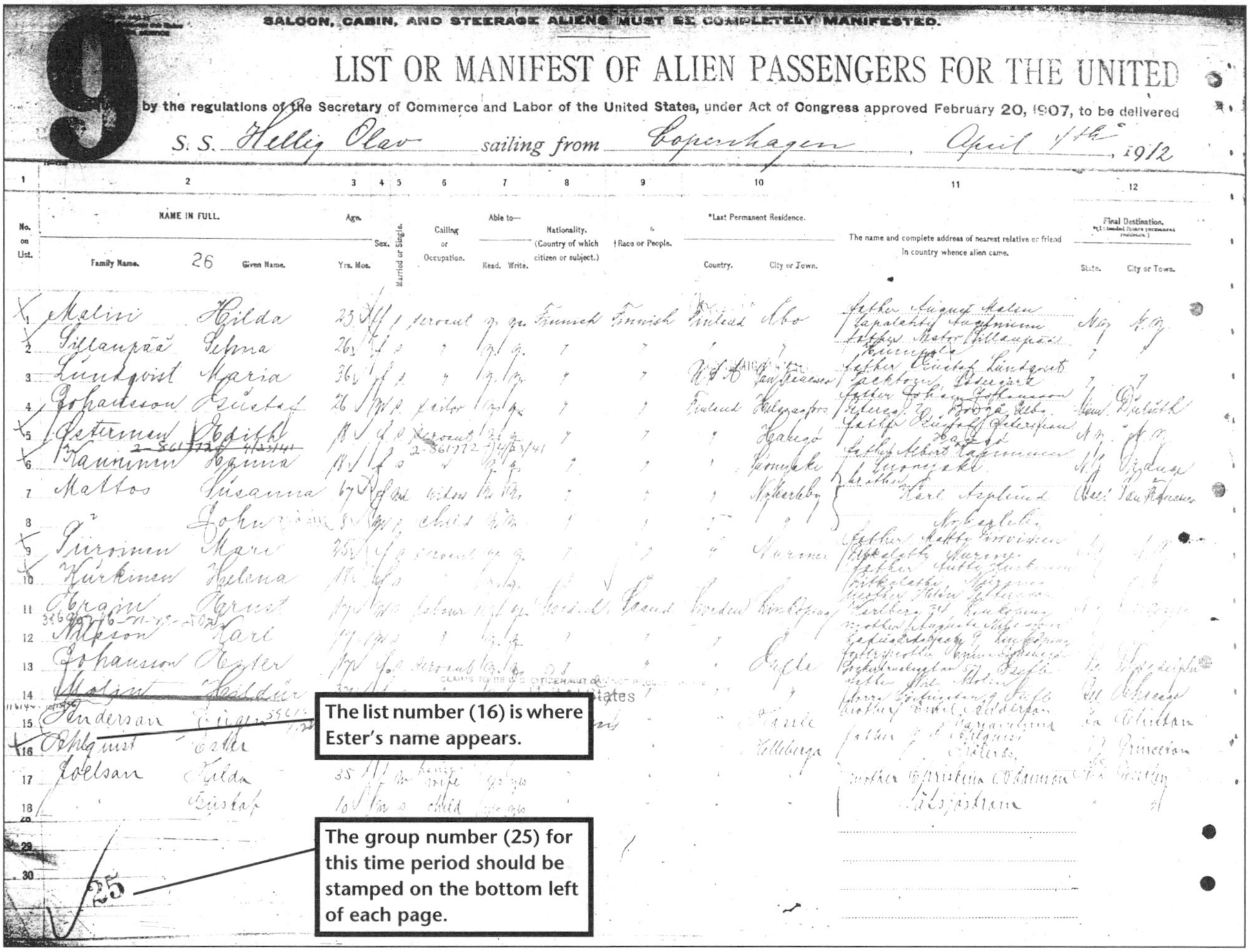

The list number (16) is where Ester's name appears.

The group number (25) for this time period should be stamped on the bottom left of each page.

Figure 4-8
In 1912 when Ester's ship arrived in New York, the group number (25) should be stamped on the bottom left of each passenger list page. Once you find this number, you'll go to the list (or line) number 16, and that's where Ester's name appears.

- Whether entering by reason of any offer: no
- Condition of Health, Mental and Physical: good
- Deformed or crippled: no
- Height: 5′4″
- Complexion: healthy
- Color of hair: dark; eyes: blue
- Marks of Identification: no
- Place of birth: Country: Sweden, City or Town: Lenhofda [Lenhovda?]

Before I make a photocopy of the pages or put the film away, I next check the end of the lists to see if Ester is on the Record of Detained Aliens (see Figure 4-10 on page 57). She should be, since most unescorted women arriving in the early twentieth century were detained until someone arrived to claim them. She's there on line 9, along with more information about her:

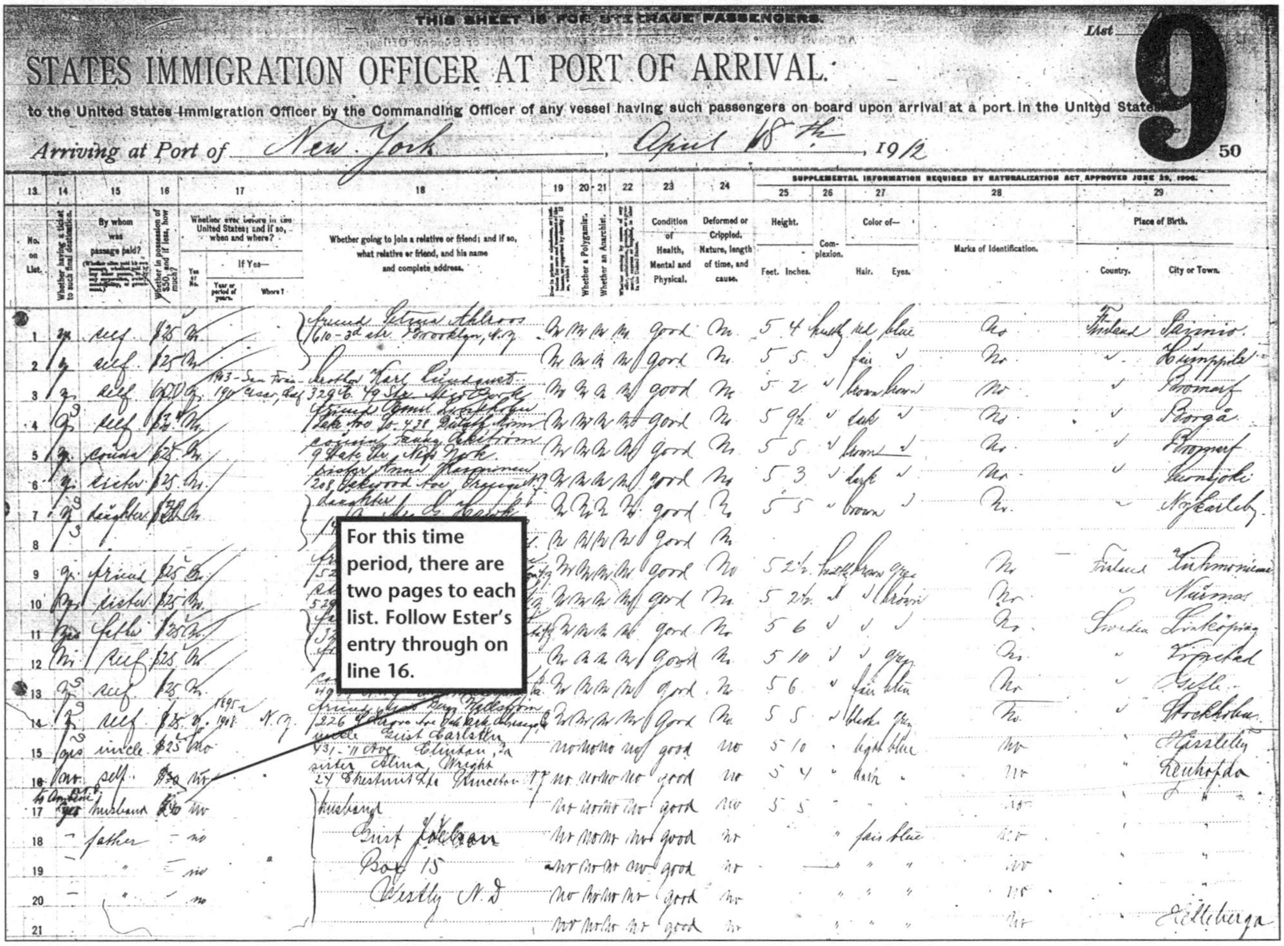

Figure 4-9
The second page of the passenger arrival list (manifest) gives more information on Ester and her fellow passengers.

The callout on the manifest reads:
> For this time period, there are two pages to each list. Follow Ester's entry through on line 16.

- Name: Ahlquist, Ester
- Manifest: Group: 9, Line: 16
- Number of Aliens: One year old or under: [none], Older than one year: 1
- Cause of Detention: To sister
- Disposition: Sister, Alrma [or Almira] Wright, 24 Chestnut St., Princeton, NJ
- Discharged: By Inspector "J," Date: 18 [April], Time: 105
  Meals: [none]

Tip

If you happen upon microfilm that is difficult to read, take the information you have from the microfilm index and go to the Ellis Island database or Morse search form to find the record on the Ellis Island database, where the images have been digitally enhanced. As you can see from Figures 4-11 and 4-12 on page 58, showing the arrival list for Annie Moore, the first immigrant to be processed through Ellis Island, the microfilmed version is difficult to read, but the enhanced and enlarged digitized version is quite clear.

FIRST- AND SECOND-CLASS PASSENGERS

The first- and second-class passengers were recorded in a separate section of the same list for a given ship. If you are cranking microfilm, you'll find a page or two for the first-class passengers first, then a few pages for the second- or saloon-class, then multiple pages for the steerage- or third-class. After that, you'd find those held for detention, then those held for the Board of Special Inquiry. If you're using online passenger lists, these pages may be in reverse order.

Just as using the Ellis Island database has some tricks to it, so do passenger lists and their indexes. Using both online and microfilmed resources can be your ticket to finding your immigrant ancestors. But what if you're still coming up empty? Let's look at some ways to overcome your brick wall.

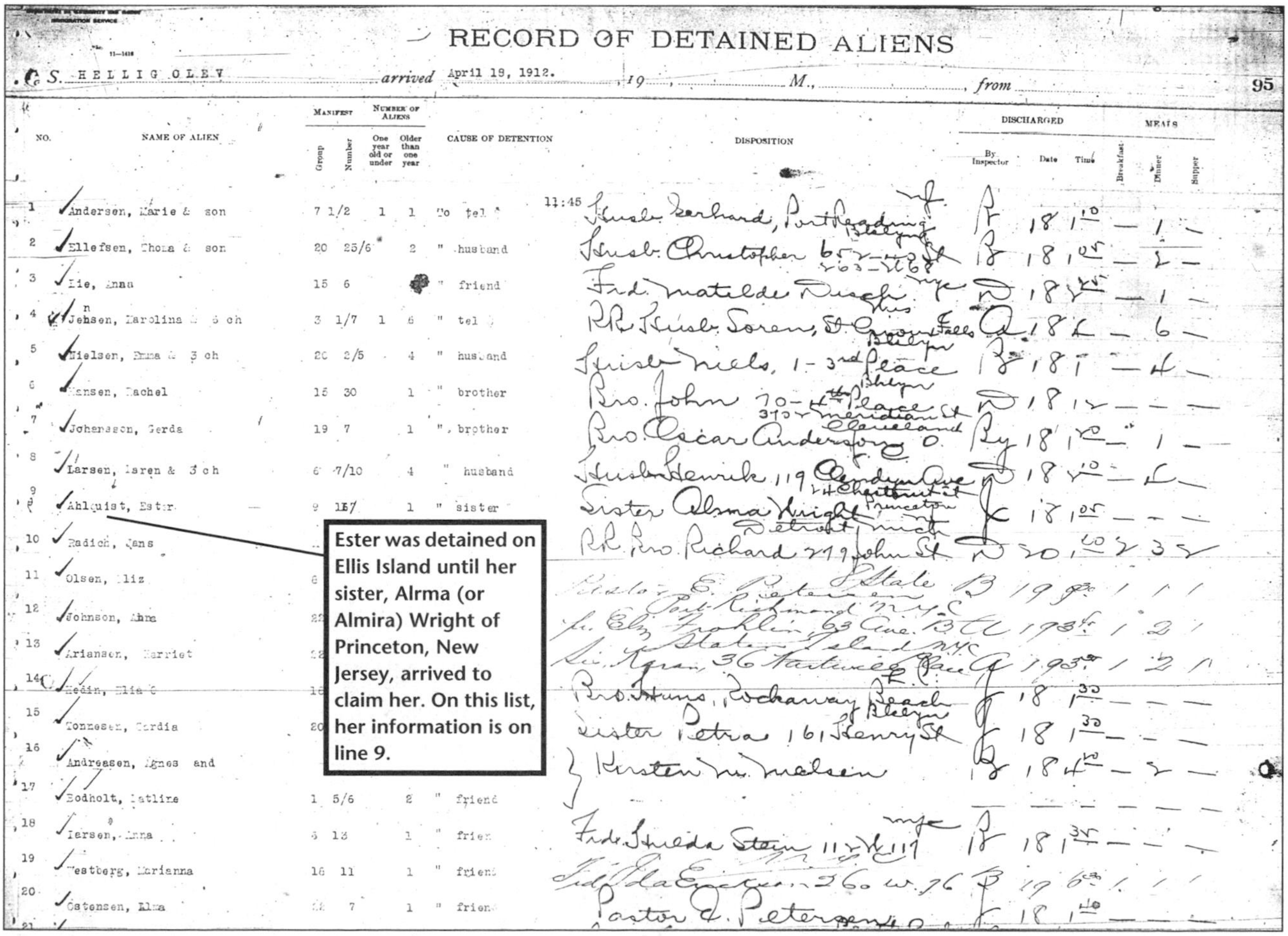

Figure 4-10
Record of detained aliens, *Hellig Olav*, NARA microfilm T715, roll 1843, volume 4085.

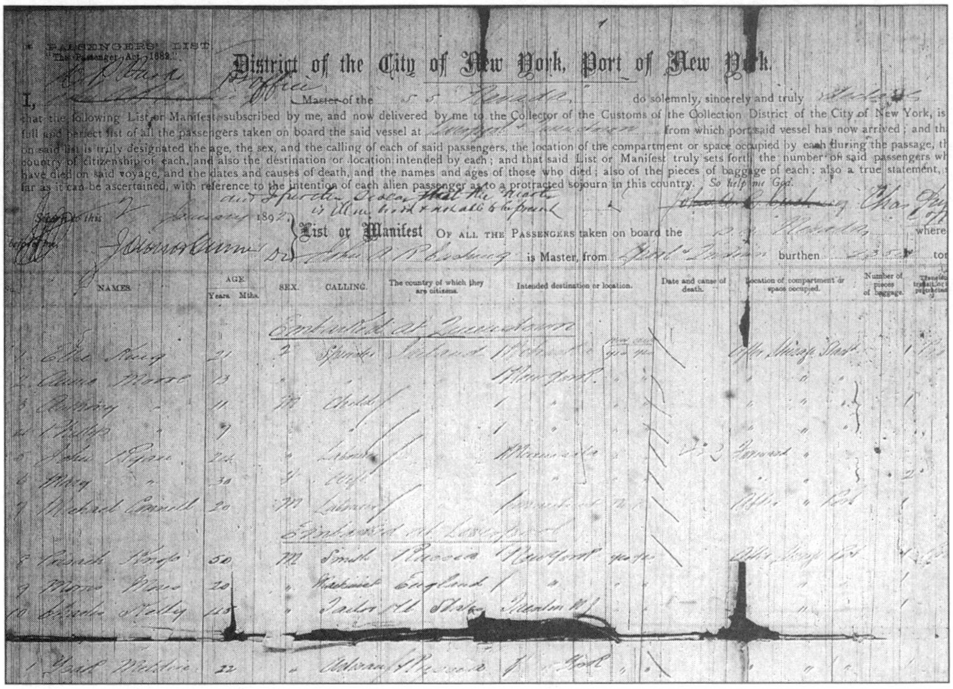

Figure 4-11
Notice how the microfilmed list showing Annie Moore's arrival (line 2) on the Nevada, 2 January 1892, is almost impossible to read. Now compare with Figure 4-12, the section of the computerized enhancement from the Ellis Island database.

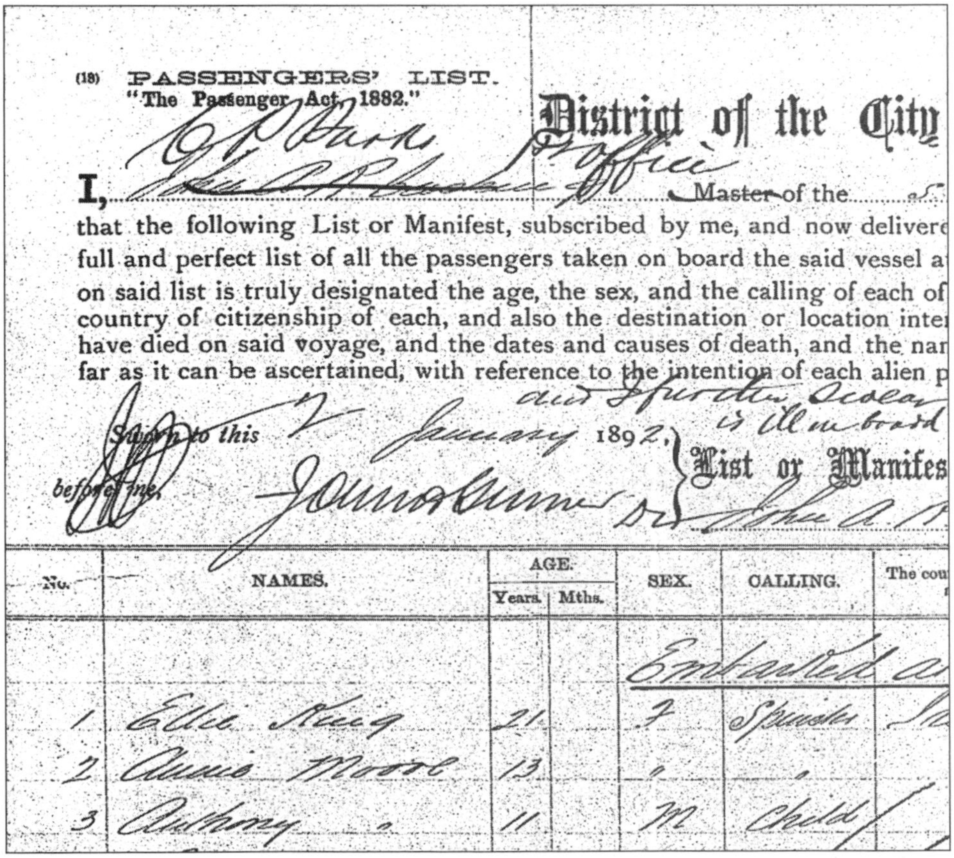

(18) PASSENGERS' LIST.
"The Passenger Act, 1882."

District of the City

I, ... Master of the ......
that the following List or Manifest, subscribed by me, and now delivere
full and perfect list of all the passengers taken on board the said vessel a
on said list is truly designated the age, the sex, and the calling of each of
country of citizenship of each, and also the destination or location inte
have died on said voyage, and the dates and causes of death, and the nar
far as it can be ascertained, with reference to the intention of each alien p

Sworn to this ... January 1892,
before me,

List or Manifes

No.	NAMES.	AGE. Years.	AGE. Mths.	SEX.	CALLING.	The cou
1	Ellie King	21		F	Spinster	
2	Annie Moore	13		"	"	
3	Anthony "	11		M	Child	

Figure 4-12
Section of enhanced computerized list for the *Nevada*, showing Annie Moore on line 2, from the Ellis Island database.

ANNIE MOORE—ELLIS ISLAND'S FIRST ARRIVAL

Sources, all of them undocumented, disagree on what happened to Annie Moore and her brothers after she left Ellis Island. One source says she "went on to become a true American, later marrying, moving west, and bearing first-generation American citizens" (Statue of Liberty National Monument, American Park Network <www.americanparknetwork.com/parkinfo/sl/history/annie .html>). Another source claims she met up with her parents Mary and Matt Moore and older brother Tom in New York City. The family then moved to Indiana, where Annie met and married Patrick O'Connell, and they subsequently moved to Waco, Texas, and then on to Clovis, New Mexico. After her husband's death, she supposedly died in 1923 in Ft. Worth, Texas, "when she was struck and killed by . . . one of the earliest rapid transit trains linking" Ft. Worth and Dallas. (*The Story of Annie Moore*, booklet at the Cobh Heritage Centre, Cobh, County Cork, Ireland [no author, no date].) Yet another source reports that Annie and her family settled in Connecticut ("Tracing Families Through Ellis Island," by Albert J. Parisi, *New York Times*, 13 November 1988, page NJ12).

Researchers have tried to unlock the mystery of what happened to Annie Moore—as well as her origin (supposedly County Cork)—but not surprisingly, none have been successful so far. Mostly they've uncovered conflicting information. With a common Irish name like Moore, let alone a female named Annie, and living in New York City, you can certainly understand the problem.

LANDED ON ELLIS ISLAND

NEW IMMIGRATION BUILDINGS OPENED YESTERDAY.

A ROSY-CHEEKED IRISH GIRL THE FIRST REGISTERED—ROOM ENOUGH FOR ALL ARRIVALS—ONLY RAILROAD PEOPLE FIND FAULT.

The new buildings on Ellis Island constructed for the use of the Immigration Bureau were yesterday formally occupied by the officials of that department. The employes reported at an early hour, and each was shown to his place by the Superintendent or his chief clerk. Col. Weber was on the island at 9 o'clock, and went on a tour of inspection to see that everything was in readiness for the reception of the first boatload of immigrants.

There were three big steamships in the harbor waiting to land their passengers, and there was much anxiety among the new-comers to be the first landed at the new station. The honor was reserved for a little rosy-cheeked Irish girl. She was Annie Moore, fifteen years of age, lately a resident of County Cork, and yesterday one of the 148 steerage passengers landed from the Guion steamship Nevada. Her name is now distinguished by being the first registered in the book of the new landing bureau.

The steamship that brought Annie Moore arrived late Thursday night. Early yesterday morning the passengers of that vessel were placed on board the immigrant transfer boat John E. Moore. The craft was gayly decorated with bunting and ranged alongside the wharf on Ellis Island amid a clang of bells and din of shrieking whistles.

As soon as the gangplank was run ashore, Annie tripped across it and was hurried into the big building that almost covers the entire island. By a prearranged plan she was escorted to a registry desk which was temporarily occupied by Mr. Charles M. Hendley, the former private secretary of Secretary Windom. He asked as a special favor the privilege of registering the first immigrant, and Col. Weber granted the request.

Figure 4-13
Statue of Annie Moore and her brothers, Philip and Anthony, located at their port of departure in Queenstown (now Cobh), Ireland, and an article from *The New York Times* announcing the opening of Ellis Island and Annie Moore as the first immigrant processed at the new receiving station (*New York Times*, 2 January 1892, page 2). She left Ireland in December 1891 and arrived at the Port of New York on 2 January 1892.

CHAPTER 5

My Ancestor Isn't There—What Now?

Y ou would think that between the Ellis Island database, Steve Morse's search forms, and the microfilmed indexes and lists you'd be able to find your ancestor using at least one of them. Sometimes ancestors continue to be elusive for one reason or another. The explanation may be that you still don't have the correct original name, right arrival year, or exact age. Or, the name simply isn't recorded as you are expecting it to be. Some other avenues of approach are still available if you are coming up empty-handed. First, ask yourself these two questions:

1. Did your ancestor indeed come through Ellis Island? Because Ellis Island was the leading immigrant receiving station of its day, many people think their ancestor came through the Port of New York, when they might have come through one of the other major U.S. ports (see "Some Ports of Arrival Other Than New York" on page 61) or Canada. Going back to Angela Vallarelli from chapter three, she had six siblings who all immigrated to America, presumably through Ellis Island. I could find them all but two. After wearing down my teeth from grinding them each time I'd get a negative search result on the Ellis Island database, I began to wonder if they might have come through another port. Sure enough, those two came through the Port of Boston, not New York.

2. Are you checking for immigrant women under their maiden names? While this custom was more prevalent in Catholic countries, it never hurts to try this strategy even if your ancestor wasn't Catholic. Regardless of whether the woman was traveling alone, with her spouse, or with her children, the woman might be recorded on the list by her maiden name. Don't know what her maiden name was? If she traveled with her children, they should be recorded under the father's surname. So look for the kids.

SOME PORTS OF ARRIVAL OTHER THAN NEW YORK

For a complete list of ports of entry by state or district, go to "Ports of Entry and Their Records" on the U.S. Citizenship and Immigration Services site <http://uscis.gov/graphics/aboutus/history/poelist/poe.htm>. See also "US Ports of Arrival and Their Available Passenger Lists 1820–1957, includes Canadian & Mexican Border Crossing Records" <www.genesearch.com/ports.html>.

Baltimore, Maryland	Key West, Florida
Boston, Massachusetts	New Bedford, Massachusetts
New Orleans, Louisiana	Portland, Maine
Philadelphia, Pennsylvania	Providence, Rhode Island
Detroit, Michigan	San Francisco, California
Galveston, Texas	Savannah, Georgia
Gloucester, Massachusetts	Seattle, Washington
Gulfport and Pascagoula, Mississippi	

FINDING AIDS

Long before the Ellis Island database was launched, kindhearted genealogists who had problems finding their own ancestors took on transcription and indexing projects for whole ships or certain ethnic groups, then published the results. **Let's look at some of these; one might be the ticket to helping you.**

Morton Allan Directory

The *Morton Allan Directory of European Passenger Steamship Arrivals for the Years 1890 to 1930 at the Port of New York and for the Years 1904 to 1926 at the Ports of New York, Philadelphia, Boston, and Baltimore* can be an extremely helpful source if your ancestors arrived during these time periods and through one of these ports. Suppose from family stories or a naturalization record you learn that your ancestor arrived in the summer of 1896 at the Port of New York on the ship *Rotterdam*. With this information, you could search on Morse's site under the ships lists, or you can search all passenger lists for that season to find the *Rotterdam*'s list, but you would be cranking through more rolls of microfilm than you'd care to count. To narrow your search, you need a precise date or at least a month. Turn to the *Morton Allan Directory*, which can be found in most genealogical libraries.

This book is arranged by year, then by the shipping lines and routes, and lists ships and their dates of arrival to a particular port. Turning to 1896,

Sources

50   MORTON ALLAN DIRECTORY

Year 1896

HAMBURG-AMERICAN LINE Scandinavian Ports—New York (Continued)		HOLLAND-AMERICA LINE Rotterdam, Amsterdam, Boulogne—New York (Continued)		LINHA DE VAPORES PORTUGUEZES Azores, Lisbon—New Bedford, Mass., New York (Continued)	
N.Y. Arrival	**Steamer**	**N.Y. Arrival**	**Steamer**	**N.Y. Arrival**	**Steamer**
May 16	Venetia	Aug. 10	Obdam	Oct. 14	Oevenum
June 6	Georgia	Aug. 15	Maasdam	Oct. 19	Dona Amelia
June 17	Virginia	Aug. 17	Zaandam	Nov. 25	Dona Maria
July 2	Venetia	Aug. 24	Spaarndam		
July 28	Georgia	Aug. 31	Amsterdam	**NATIONAL NAVIGATION COMPANY**	
Aug. 7	Virginia	Aug. 31	Schiedam	Mediterranean—New York	
Sept. 15	Georgia	Sept. 3	Werkendam	**N.Y. Arrival**	**Steamer**
Sept. 29	Virginia	Sept. 7	Veendam	Mar. 23	Hindoustan
Oct. 13	Venetia	Sept. 8	Rotterdam	May 9	Chamdernager
Nov. 5	Georgia	Sept. 11	Edam		
Nov. 16	Virginia	Sept. 14	Obdam	**NORTH GERMAN LLOYD**	
Dec. 3	Venetia	Sept. 21	Maasdam	Bremen—New York	
		Sept. 28	Spaarndam	**N.Y. Arrival**	**Steamer**
HOLLAND-AMERICA LINE		Oct. 3	Zaandam	Jan. 6	Bonn
Rotterdam, Amsterdam, Boulogne—New York		Oct. 7	Amsterdam	Jan. 10	Weimar
N.Y. Arrival	**Steamer**	Oct. 10	Veendam	Jan. 16	Aller
Jan. 2	Schiedam	Oct. 13	Schiedam	Jan. 18	Stuttgart
Jan. 13	Zaandam	Oct. 13	Rotterdam	Jan. 28	Aachen
Jan. 18	Rotterdam	Oct. 16	Werkendam	Feb. 3	Willehad
Jan. 21	Werkendam	Oct. 19	Obdam	Feb. 6	Spree
Jan. 23	Veendam	Oct. 24	Maasdam	Feb. 12	Braunschweig
Jan. 27	Spaarndam	Oct. 26	Edam	Feb. 15	Aller
Feb. 5	Amsterdam	Nov. 2	Spaarndam	Feb. 20	Munchen
Feb. 10	Maasdam	Nov. 9	Veendam	Feb. 21	Havel
Feb. 21	Edam	Nov. 16	Zaandam	Feb. 24	Weimar
Feb. 24	Schiedam	Nov. 18	Rotterdam	Mar. 2	Halle
Feb. 27	Rotterdam	Nov. 20	Werkendam	Mar. 3	Dresden
Feb. 27	Werkendam	Nov. 24	Obdam	Mar. 6	Spree
Mar. 10	Amsterdam	Dec. 3	Schiedam	Mar. 7	Stuttgart
Mar. 16	Veendam	Dec. 7	Maasdam	Mar. 13	Saale
Mar. 19	Zaandam	Dec. 9	Edam	Mar. 17	Aachen
Mar. 23	Maasdam	Dec. 15	Spaarndam	Mar. 19	Havel
Apr. 2	Rotterdam	Dec. 26	Werkendam	Mar. 21	H. H. Meier
Apr. 2	Edam	Dec. 28	Veendam	Mar. 27	Aller
Apr. 7	Spaarndam	Dec. 28	Rotterdam	Mar. 31	Bonn
Apr. 9	Schiedam	Dec. 30	Zaandam	Apr. 2	Spree
Apr. 14	Amsterdam			Apr. 9	Lahn
Apr. 20	Veendam	**INSULAR NAVIGATION COMPANY**		Apr. 10	Halle
Apr. 27	Zaandam	Azores, Lisbon—New Bedford, Mass., New York		Apr. 14	Saale
Apr. 27	Maasdam	**N.Y. Arrival**	**Steamer**	Apr. 16	Havel
May 4	Werkendam	Mar. 16	Peninsular	Apr. 16	Stuttgart
May 11	Spaarndam	May 5	Peninsular	Apr. 27	Aller
May 11	Rotterdam	June 22	Peninsular	Apr. 27	Aachen
May 18	Amsterdam	Aug. 10	Peninsular	Apr. 29	H. H. Meier
May 25	Veendam	Sept. 28	Peninsular	May 1	Spree
May 27	Schiedam	Nov. 20	Peninsular	May 7	Lahn
June 5	Zaandam	Nov. 28	Vega	May 11	Bonn
June 8	Maasdam			May 12	Saale
June 12	Werkendam	**LINHA DE VAPORES PORTUGUEZES**		May 13	Dresden
June 15	Spaarndam	Azores, Lisbon—New Bedford, Mass., New York		May 14	Havel
June 23	Amsterdam	**N.Y. Arrival**	**Steamer**	May 21	Trave
June 29	Edam	Jan. 30	Oevenum	May 22	Halle
June 29	Veendam	Mar. 30	Dona Maria	May 25	Aller
July 6	Obdam	Mar. 30	Oevenum	May 27	Stuttgart
July 13	Maasdam	May 25	Oevenum	May 28	Spree
July 22	Rotterdam	July 14	Oevenum	June 4	Aachen
July 24	Werkendam	Aug. 21	Dona Maria	June 4	Lahn
July 27	Amsterdam			June 8	Saale
Aug. 3	Veendam			June 10	H. H. Meier
Aug. 5	Edam			June 11	Havel

> The *Rotterdam* arrives in New York.

Figure 5-1

Morton Allan Directory of European Passenger Steamship Arrivals. The *Rotterdam* sailed for the Holland-America Line.

you can scan the lists of ships' names and find that the *Rotterdam*, which sailed under the Holland-America Line, docked in New York nine times that year, but it arrived only once during the summer months, on 22 July 1896 (see Figure 5-1 on page 62).

Sometimes other genealogical records will give you a precise arrival date, but the date could be off by a few days, so double-check the date in the *Morton Allan Directory*. Keep in mind also that this directory gives the dates the ships were scheduled to arrive, not the actual arrival date. Delays of a few days were common. Also, this directory is not complete regarding steamships arriving from Europe, and it does not list ships arriving from places other than Europe.

Published Passenger Lists by Ethnicity

Several volumes of books divide ethnic groups by their arrival. While you should be able to find the printed works in large genealogical libraries, some are now available for purchase on CD-ROM through Genealogical Publishing Company, <www.genealogical.com/default.asp>:

Germans to America, 1850–1874 Passenger & Immigration Lists

Germans to America, 1875–1888 Passenger & Immigration Lists

Irish to America Passenger & Immigration Lists, Vol. 2, 1846–1886

Irish to America, 1846–1865: Passenger & Immigration Lists

Italians to America, 1880–1893 Passenger & Immigration Lists

Books

Baca, Leo. *Czech Immigration Passenger Lists*. Comp. 7 vols. Richardson, Tex.: the author, 1983–1999.

Glazier, Ira A. *The Famine Immigrants: Lists of Irish Immigrants Arriving at the Port of New York, 1846–1851*. 7 vols. Baltimore: Genealogical Publishing Co., 1983–1986.

———. *Migration from the Russian Empire: Lists of Passengers Arriving at the Port of New York*. 6 vols. Baltimore: Genealogical Publishing Co., 1995–1997.

Glazier, Ira A., and P. William Filby. *Germans to America: Lists of Passengers Arriving at U.S. Ports*. 67+ volumes. Wilmington, Del.: Scholarly Resources, 1988–2002.

———. *Italians to America: Lists of Passengers Arriving at U.S. Ports, 1880–1899*. 16 vols. Wilmington, Del.: Scholarly Resources, 1992–2002.

Index to Emigrants from Sweden to New York, 1851–1869. Salt Lake City: Genealogical Society of Utah, 1987–1988.

Olsen, Nils William, and Erik Wikén. *Swedish Passenger Arrivals in the United States, 1820–1850*. Stockholm: Schmidts Boktryckeri AB, 1995.

IF NOT NEW YORK, WHERE?

In the nineteenth century, five major ports of arrival received significant numbers of newcomers: Baltimore, Boston, New Orleans, New York, and Philadelphia, with New York seeing three-quarters of all arrivals by the 1880s (and which is why it gets so much attention). Also in use throughout the nineteenth and well into the twentieth century were more than ninety other ports on the Atlantic, Pacific, Gulf Coast, and Great Lakes. (See "Some Ports of Arrival Other Than New York" on page 61.)

To say that most Germans or Italians or Irish favored one port of arrival over another would be misleading, as each ethnic group arrived through all the ports. Oftentimes, their port destination was determined by what they could afford for passage, when the next ship was leaving, where relatives had already settled, and where they had heard they could find work. For example, while the greatest influx of Italians came through the port of New York, significant numbers also came through New Orleans, Philadelphia, Baltimore, and Boston. The same with other ethnic arrivals.

Most original passenger arrival lists, 1820–1957 (with some gaps), have been microfilmed and are available through the National Archives, and these are also available through the Family History Library in Salt Lake City, Utah, and its Family History Centers. The regional records services facilities of the National Archives have films for the ports in their jurisdiction.

Here are the other four major ports and time periods that have microfilmed indexes:

Baltimore	1820–1897, 1833–1866, 1897–1952
Boston	1848–1891, 1902–1906, 1906–1920
New Orleans	1853–1899, 1900–1952
Philadelphia	1800–1906, 1883–1948

The guide *Immigrant and Passenger Arrivals: A Select Catalog of National Archives Microfilm Publications* details more fully the availability of records and indexes for each port. This catalog is available on the Internet via the National Archives' Web site at <www.archives.gov/publications/microfilm_catalogs/immigrant/im migrant_passenger_arrivals.html>, or you should be able to locate a copy at most genealogical libraries.

Swierenga, Robert P. *Dutch Immigrants in U.S. Ship Passenger Manifests, 1820–1880: An Alphabetical Listing by Household Heads and Independent Persons.* 2 vols. Wilmington, Del.: Scholarly Resources, 1983.

Voultsos, Mary. *Greek Immigrant Passengers, 1885–1910.* Comp. 4 vols. Worcester, Mass.: the author, 1991.

OTHER WEB SITES

A good starting portal is Cyndi's List, "Ports of Entry" <www.cyndislist.com/portse ntry.htm> and "Ships and Passenger Lists" <www.cyndislist.com/ships.htm>. If you don't find enough to look at under those categories, also check under the topics of "Immigration and Naturalization" and "Ports of Departure."

In your favorite search engine, such as Google, type in *"passenger lists" + New York* to check for additional sites that offer passenger databases. One of particular note is the Immigrant Ships Transcribers Guild <www.immigran tships.net>. This group of volunteers makes ships' passenger lists available online, at no cost to the user. They have transcribed more than 5,000 ships' passenger lists, covering more than half a million passenger arrivals, but not every ship has been done, of course. For New York, the transcribed lists cover 1710–1939. You need to check the site to see if the ship your ancestor came on has been transcribed yet, and more are being added all the time.

Internet Source

Figure 5-2
The Immigrant Ships Transcribers Guild is a volunteer site. Click on their Captain's Log to find out the names of ships currently being transcribed.

Another place to check is Ancestry.com's U.S. Immigration database, which is available by subscription only. Along with New York arrivals for 1851–1891 (these are the Castle Garden years; see chapter six), you'll find the Passenger and Immigration Lists Index, 1500s–1900s. Updated annually, this index contains more than four million people who arrived in the United States and Canada.

STILL STUCK?

If after checking all these possibilities you still can't find your ancestor, perhaps you need to review information you've already gathered and also see if you can find additional American sources that might offer some clues. Here's a reminder of five sources to check:

1. *Family Stories.* Because Ellis Island was the leading immigrant receiving station of its day, many people think their ancestor came through the Port of New York, when the ancestor might have come

For More Info

Emily Anne Croom's *The Genealogist's Companion and Sourcebook*, 2d ed. (Cincinnati: Betterway Books, 2003), will help you find and use the sources discussed here.

through one of the other major U.S. ports or Canada. If relatives say your ancestor came through Ellis Island, but you aren't having any luck with the Ellis Island database and corresponding microfilmed indexes, try other ports. Do a process of elimination by checking the indexes of the major ports first.

Family members may have letters, diaries, photographs of the ship an ancestor came on, or other mementos passed down through the years that would provide clues. Be sure to ask for these items. Sometimes, something that may not seem important to them is a big help to you, or they may have forgotten they had these items in their possession.

Also be sure to ask what the immigrant's original name was before he or she came to this country. This is the name that will likely appear on the ship's list. Remember, the lists were compiled at the port of departure, and immigrants used their names from the Old Country. It's not until they begin assimilating into American society that they will change their names (either to blend in or because others had difficulty pronouncing their names).

Besides knowing the immigrant ancestor's original name, you'll also

ANGEL ISLAND, "ELLIS ISLAND OF THE WEST"

Opening in 1910 in the area known as China Cove in San Francisco Bay, Angel Island <www.angelisland.org/immigr02.html> became the immigrant receiving station for the West. The function of this immigration station was to control the flow of Chinese entering the country, who were officially not welcome when the Chinese Exclusion Act was passed in 1882.

The National Archives microfilmed a variety of records for the Port of San Francisco. (For more record groups, see *Immigrant and Passenger Arrivals: A Select Catalog of National Archives Microfilm Publications.*)

- Indexes to Passenger Lists of Vessels Arriving at San Francisco, California, 1893–1934. M1389. 28 rolls.

- Passenger Lists of Vessels Arriving at San Francisco, 1893–1953, M1410. 429 rolls.

- Registers of Chinese Laborers Returning to the U.S. through the Port of San Francisco, 1882–1888, M1413. 12 rolls.

- Lists of Chinese Passenger Arrivals at San Francisco, 1882–1914, M1414. 32 rolls.

- Lists of Chinese Applying for Admission to the United States through the Port of San Francisco, 1903–1947, M1476. 27 rolls.

need to know his approximate age at the time of departure from the homeland and the approximate date (year) of arrival in America.

2. *Censuses*. If family stories don't give you a clue as to when the immigrant ancestor arrived, check every census on which the ancestor might be listed. The first census to give clues to immigration was 1870, asking each person if parents were foreign born. Later censuses give years of arrival and naturalization:

1880 birthplace of person and parents

1900 birthplace of person and parents; if foreign born, year of immigration and whether naturalized; ability to speak English

1910 birthplace and mother tongue of person and parents; if foreign born, year of immigration, whether naturalized, and whether able to speak English, and if not, language spoken

1920 if foreign born, year of immigration to the United States, whether naturalized, and year of naturalization; birthplace of person and parents; mother tongue of foreign born; ability to speak English

1930 birthplace of person and parents; if foreign born, language spoken in home before coming to the United States, year of immigration, whether naturalized, and ability to speak English

Keep in mind that the year of immigration given in the census may not be accurate, as we don't know who provided that information to the census taker. Even if the immigrant herself gave the date of arrival, she could be off by a year or two.

Remember to look for state censuses as well as federal censuses. Sometimes state censuses give more detailed information about immigration. The New York state censuses for the early twentieth century, for example, not only asked for year of immigration and whether naturalized, but they also asked for the court/city in which the immigrant was naturalized. See Ann S. Lainhart's *State Census Records* (Baltimore: Genealogical Publishing Co., 2000) for a state-by-state listing of these schedules, what type of information they contain, and their availability.

3. *City Directories*. A city directory is an alphabetical list of inhabitants in a given locality that predates telephone directories and gives more information, such as occupation. Tracing immigrants backward in city directories may be helpful in pinpointing an approximate year of ar-

CANADIAN BORDER CROSSINGS

Many immigrant families arrived through Canadian ports, some settling for a time in Canada before coming to the United States. No records on those who crossed the border were kept by the United States until 1895, when the United States government realized that about 40 percent of those who arrived in Canada had as their final destination the United States. Joint immigrant inspection between Canada and the United States created two sets of records: passenger lists and inspection cards. Records from all ports of entry within the INS Montreal district were centralized at the district headquarters in Montreal (later St. Albans, Vermont). The records and Soundex have been microfilmed and are available at the National Archives, at all the regional records services facilities of the National Archives, and through the Family History Library in Salt Lake City.

- Soundex Index to Canadian Border Entries through the St. Albans, Vermont, District, 1895–1924.

- Soundex Index to Entries into the St. Albans, Vermont, District through Canadian Pacific and Atlantic Ports, 1924–1952.

- Alphabetical Index to Canadian Border Entries through Small Ports in Vermont, 1895–1924.

- Manifest of Passengers Arriving in the St. Albans, VT, District through Canadian Pacific and Atlantic Ports, 1895–1954.

- Manifest of Passengers Arriving in the St. Albans, Vermont, District through Canadian Pacific Ports, 1929–1949.

Like the Soundex cards for ships' passenger arrival lists to the United States, the index cards for Canadian border crossings are on microfilm and arranged by the Soundex code, then alphabetically by the passenger's first name. Each card contains an abstract of the information found on the manifest. The Soundex covering 1895–1924 also includes names of people who crossed through other United States borders within the Montreal district: Washington, Montana, Michigan, New York, North Dakota, and Minnesota.

The actual manifests, 1895–1954, contain two types of lists: a traditional passenger arrival list of seaports, and monthly lists of names of aliens crossing the land border, usually on trains. The monthly lists are arranged by month and year, then alphabetically by the name of the port, then by the name of the railway. For more information, see Constance Potter, "St. Albans Passenger Arrival Records," in *Prologue* 22 (Spring 1990): 90-93.

rival, but immigrants may not appear in city directories for several years after their arrival, or they may appear sporadically. Historical demographers have noted that most urban immigrant families had a high mobility rate, moving about every ten years once in America, regardless of whether it was across the nation, across town, or across the street.

4. *Obituaries and Death Certificates*. Oftentimes you can find an immigrant ancestor's place of origin and when he came to America in his obituary. Likewise, some state's death certificates may ask how long the deceased had been in America. Keep in mind, however, that the immigrant himself did not supply the information, so use arrival dates or origins listed in obituaries and death certificates as starting places.

5. *Military Draft Records*. Most genealogists think to look for military records, but they often overlook draft records, which can hold a wealth of clues about your immigrant ancestors. They, too, had to register for the draft, regardless of their citizenship status. **The draft records most relevant to the Ellis Island years are for World War I.**

Sources

The government held three draft registrations for World War I: one in 1917 and two in 1918. More than twenty-four million men between the ages of eighteen and forty-five registered, including naturalized citizens and aliens, although not all were inducted into service. Registration cards may include the registrant's name, age, date and place of birth, home address, race, citizenship, occupation, personal description, and prior military service.

WWI draft records are arranged alphabetically by state, then by county or city (except cards for Connecticut, Massachusetts, and Rhode Island, which are arranged alphabetically by registrant). To obtain the registration record for a man who lived in a rural area, you need only to know his name and the county where he registered. For a man who resided in a major city, you must know the registrant's street address because these cities had several draft boards. To locate someone's address, consult city directories.

Original World War I draft records are located at the National Archives' Southeast Region in East Point, Georgia. They're also available on microfilm through the Church of Jesus Christ of Latter-day Saints' Family History Library (FHL) <www.familysearch.org> in Salt Lake City or through its branch Family History Centers (FHCs). To find the FHC nearest you, visit <www.familysearch.org/eng/Library/FHC/frameset_fhc.asp>. You can search the FHL's catalog online by clicking on the Search tab and then Family History Library Catalog. Once you've found microfilm that interests you, request it through the library or your FHC. You can also access some state's World War I draft records on Ancestry.com (by subscription). More states are being added.

Figure 5-3
World War I draft registration of Rudolf Triepitsch, Wisconsin, Milwaukee Draft Board #5, FHL 1674784. More than twenty-four million men registered for the draft during World War I. Regardless of whether a man was an alien or citizen, he was supposed to register. (The second page of this registration is not shown.)

Recorded is the citizenship status (a natural-born citizen, a naturalized citizen, an alien, or declared intention).

Also recorded are the town, state, and nation of the person's birth.

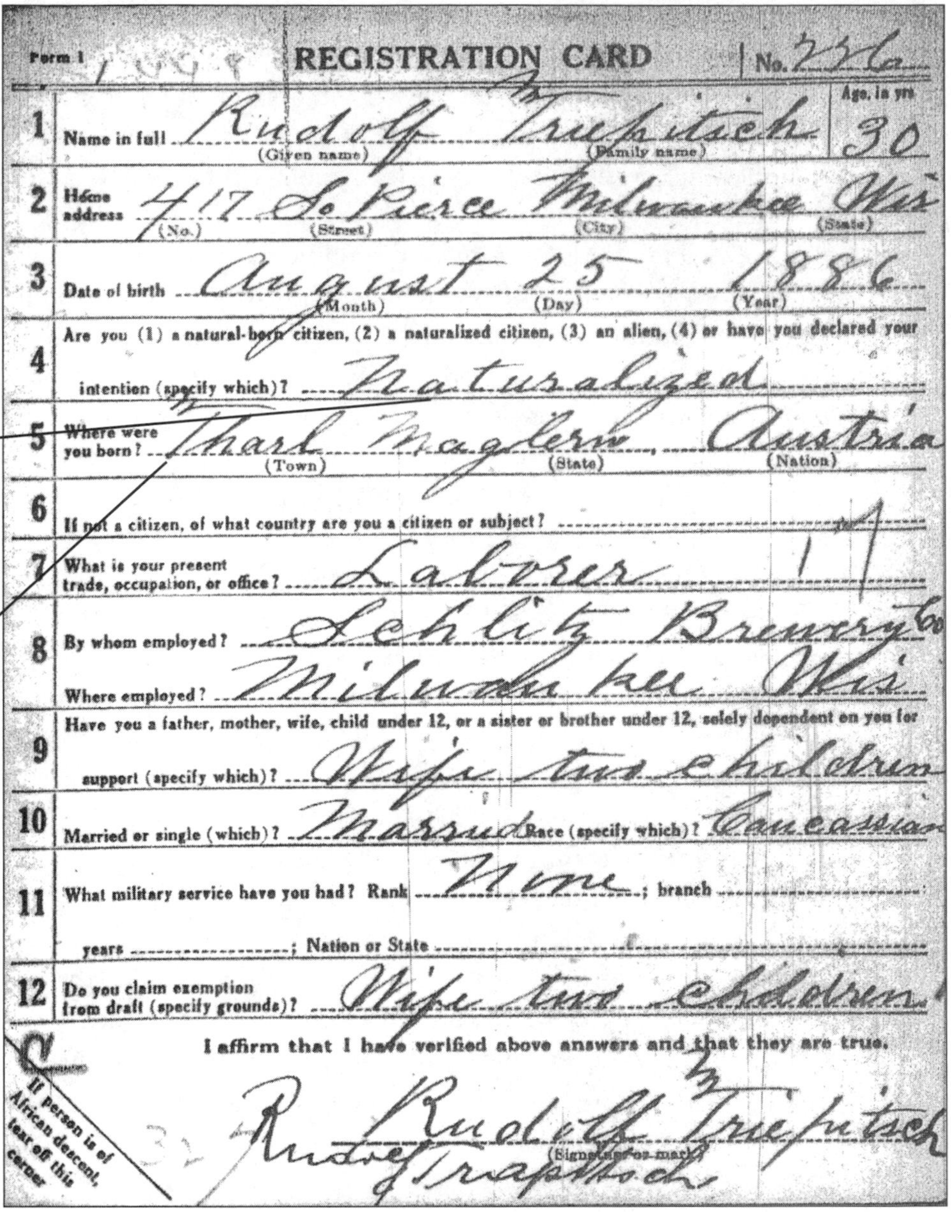
Form 1 REGISTRATION CARD No. 236

1 Name in full Rudolf Triepitsch (Given name) (Family name) Age, in yrs. 30

2 Home address 417 So Pierce Milwaukee Wis (No.) (Street) (City) (State)

3 Date of birth August 25 1886 (Month) (Day) (Year)

4 Are you (1) a natural-born citizen, (2) a naturalized citizen, (3) an alien, (4) or have you declared your intention (specify which)? Naturalized

5 Where were you born? Tharl Maglern Austria (Town) (State) (Nation)

6 If not a citizen, of what country are you a citizen or subject?

7 What is your present trade, occupation, or office? Labrer

8 By whom employed? Schlitz Brewery Co
Where employed? Milwaukee Wis

9 Have you a father, mother, wife, child under 12, or a sister or brother under 12, solely dependent on you for support (specify which)? Wife two children

10 Married or single (which)? Married Race (specify which)? Caucasian

11 What military service have you had? Rank None; branch
years ; Nation or State

12 Do you claim exemption from draft (specify grounds)? Wife two children

I affirm that I have verified above answers and that they are true.

Rudolf Triepitsch (Signature or mark)

If person is of African descent, tear off this corner

DILIGENCE PAYS OFF

As a final resort, assuming you know at least the month and year of arrival and the name of the ship, you may want to read the entire passenger list. Names that are difficult to read or hard for the transcriber or indexer to decipher may actually be there for you to find. The unfortunate reality, though, is that sometimes it's just impossible to find the arrival of some ancestors. You know they got here, but you just can't find the list. It's frustrating, to say the least. But don't give up until you've tried a variety of sources and methods.

CHAPTER 6

Before Ellis Island: Castle Garden

P rior to the mid-nineteenth century, the United States had no immigrant inspection stations. Then in 1855, Castle Garden opened, located on the southern tip of Manhattan. Here, short inspections and medical examinations of arriving passengers took place. More than eight million newcomers entered through Castle Garden, which gave way to Ellis Island in 1892.

CASTLE GARDEN HISTORY

Known in the early 1800s as Castle Clinton, named after Mayor DeWitt Clinton, the area housed a fort with twenty-eight cannons and eight-foot-

Figure 6-1
Castle Garden. Photo courtesy of the Ellis Island Immigration Museum.

thick walls. In 1824, the fort became known as Castle Garden, and for three decades it was New York City's place for the affluent to attend celebrity galas and concerts, watch fireworks, and attend political rallies. The year following its change in venue, the old fort was one of the first public buildings to have gas lighting. By 1844, it received a roof and an interior massive water fountain, and it became a large opera house and theater. In 1855, the island was joined to Manhattan by landfill. The concert hall was leased to the state, and the old fort became an immigrant receiving station. When Ellis Island replaced it, the fort was remodeled into an aquarium. Today, Castle Garden is known again as Castle Clinton <www.nps.gov/cacl>, and the National Park Service has restored the fort to its original state. It is also the place where you buy your ferry tickets for Ellis Island.

CASTLE GARDEN LISTS

Passenger lists from 1820 to about 1891 were known as customs lists, although those who had ancestors who came through New York after 1855 sometimes refer to these as the Castle Garden lists. As discussed in chapter two, the lists were generally completed by the shipping company personnel at the port of departure, then printed in the United States, and were maintained primarily for statistical purposes; therefore, the information is meager. You'll find the name of the ship and its master, port of embarkation, date and port of arrival, and each passenger's name, sex, age, occupation, and nationality. The Port of New York lists (with some gaps) have been microfilmed and are available through the National Archives, NARA's Northeast Regional facility in New York City, at the Family History Library in Salt Lake City, Utah, and its worldwide Family History Centers. **And now, they are also available online through subscription at Ancestry.com.**

Internet Source

When you subscribe and log onto Ancestry.com, click on the tab for "Search Records," then look for "Immigration Records," and click on "New York Passenger Lists." Here you can search by name, with either an exact spelling search or a Soundex search. The names are linked to the actual images of passenger lists copied from NARA's microfilm series M237, rolls 95–580. Or, if you know the month, year, and name of the ship your ancestor arrived on, scroll down and click on a year, then the month, and the name of the ship. The first page of the original manifest will appear, and then you can search through the whole manifest and print out the pages of interest.

The problem with the passenger lists for the Castle Garden years is the lists usually do not have enough identifying information to ensure that you have the correct ancestor, especially when you have one with a common name. In looking on the Ancestry.com site for Mary Gordon, for example, who was about twenty-one when she came to America in the 1850s, I found

Search Results Provided By   The No. 1 Source for Family History Online *Ancestry.com.*

Database: New York Passenger Lists, 1851-1891   January 6, 2005 12:49 AM

Match Quality	Name	Arrival Date	Estimated Birth Year	Gender	Port of Departure	Place of Origin	Destination	Ship Name	View Image
★★★☆☆	Mary Gordon	15 Dec 1851	1816	Female	Liverpool, England	Ireland	United States of America	Conway	🔍
★★★☆☆	Mary Gordon	3 Mar 1851	1830	Female	Liverpool, England	Ireland	United States of America	Guy Mannering	🔍
★★★☆☆	Mary Gordon	9 Jan 1851	1831	Female	Liverpool, England	Ireland	United States of America	Lady Hobart	🔍
★★★☆☆	Mary Gordon	4 Oct 1851	1815	Female	London, England	England	United States of America	Mississippi	🔍
★★★☆☆	Mary Gordon	6 Sep 1851	1831	Female	Liverpool, England	Co Longford	Edgeworthtown	Mortimer Livingston	🔍
★★★☆☆	Mary Gordon	16 Sep 1851	1806	Female	Liverpool, England	Ireland	United States of America	Roscius	🔍
★★★☆☆	Mary Gordon	23 Oct 1852	1827	Female	Liverpool, England	Ireland	United States of America	Meridian	🔍
★★★☆☆	Mary Gordon	23 Jul 1852	1806	Female	Liverpool, England	Ireland	United States of America	Richard Morse	🔍
★★★☆☆	Mary Gordon	2 Jun 1852	1834	Female	Liverpool, England	Ireland	United States of America	State Rights	🔍
★★★☆☆	Mary Gordon	14 May 1853	1803	Female	Liverpool, England	Ireland	United States of America	America	🔍
★★★☆☆	Mary Gordon	30 Nov 1853	1839	Female	Liverpool, England	Ireland	United States of America	Marathon	🔍
★★★☆☆	Mary Gordon	17 Oct 1853	1833	Female	Liverpool, England	Ireland		Otseonthe	🔍
★★★☆☆	Mary Gordon	17 Oct 1854	1854	Female	Liverpool, England	United States of America	United States of America	Baltic	🔍
★★★☆☆	Mary Gordon	16 May 1854	1831	Female	Liverpool, England	Ireland	United States of America	North American	🔍
★★★☆☆	Mary Gordon	28 Sep 1855	1830	Female	Liverpool, England	Great Britain	Hartford S Con	Ashburton	🔍
★★★☆☆	Mary Gordon	4 Dec 1855	1834	Female	Liverpool, England	Ireland	United States of America	City of Mobile	🔍
★★★☆☆	Mary Gordon	9 Aug 1856	1835	Female	Liverpool, England	Ireland	United States of America	Albson	🔍
★★★☆☆	Mary Gordon	7 Jul 1856	1831	Female	Liverpool, England	Great Britain	United States of America	John Bright	🔍
★★★☆☆	Mary Gordon	2 Jun 1856	1840	Female	Liverpool, England	Ireland	United States of America	Torchlight	🔍
★★★☆☆	Mary Gordon	7 Jul 1857	1807	Female	Liverpool, England	Scotland	United States of America	Constitution	🔍

Figure 6-2
Search results for Mary Gordon in New York Passenger Lists, 1851–1891 on Ancestry.com. Micropublication M237. Rolls # 95–580. National Archives, Washington, D.C.

eight possible candidates who came during this time (see Figure 6-2 above). Which one is the Mary Gordon I'm looking for? We can rule out any of them who are married, since our Mary was single when she arrived, but that still leaves several possibilities. When researching the lists for the Castle Garden years—and for a common name especially—you need to know the names of others who traveled with her, in order to correctly identify the woman you're after. Then again, the Mary we're looking for may not be any of these women, as her name might be recorded differently on the passenger list or might be mistranscribed in the database.

Let's say you have no further identifying information about Mary Gordon. Assuming the number of passengers who fit your ancestor's information is manageable, note the names of the passengers listed above and below your ancestor's name, then search for those names in conjunction with your ances-

Figure 6-3
Passenger list for the *City of Mobile*, arriving at the Port of New York on 4 December 1855. Image printed from Ancestry.com's New York Passenger Lists, 1851–1891.

tor in other records. For example, on the passenger manifest shown in Figure 6-3 above for the *City of Mobile*, you would note the names Mary Jane Gorman, 21, who appears on the line above Mary, and the three passengers below her: Mary Sullivan, 8, Johanna Blervett [?], 12, and Biddy Colbertt, 20. An eight-year-old and a twelve-year-old aren't likely traveling alone, and since they are listed right below Mary's name, the possibility is good that they are traveling with her (adults were usually listed before the children accompanying them). Now you'd review all the records you've gathered for Mary during her lifetime in America, such as censuses—or in Ireland, if you know where she came from and if the records are available. Do any of these other passenger names show up in the records? If so, then you've identified your Mary. If not, move on to the next candidate and try the same method.

MORSE'S CASTLE GARDEN SEARCH FORMS

Stephen Morse has also created his signature one-step search form for the Castle Garden years at <www.stevemorse.org/ellis/castle.html>. The search engine covers the years 1851 to 1891 and includes the following:

1851 to 1855: pre-Castle Garden

1855 to 1890: Castle Garden

1890 to 1891: Barge Office

Reminder

You'll need to subscribe to Ancestry.com for the search form to work. **Since Morse is continually adding to his massive search tools, it would be a good idea to check out his home page from time to time <www.stevemorse.org>.**

Although your Castle Garden search is easier now that the lists for that time period are online, remember you need to have enough identifying information for your ancestor to make sure you have the right person. An immigrant who has the same name as your ancestor, is from the same country, and is about the right age isn't enough—unless it's a really unusual name, and absolutely no others fit the criteria. Be cautious.

CHAPTER 7

The Immigrant Experience

Have you ever wondered what it was like for your ancestors to leave their homelands—likely never to return again—travel for two weeks aboard a crowded ship in steerage, then process along with thousands of others through Ellis Island? When you read about other immigrants' experiences, you'll realize that your ancestors had courage, endurance, a strong constitution, and an overwhelming desire for a better life.

Although your ancestors' names aren't here, their experience is. Consider what it's like to travel today: You purchase a ticket, go to the airport, process through security, board a plane, then land at another airport. It's pretty much the same experience for everyone. The same was true of your ancestors. While each journey differs in the names of the immigrants, the experience is pretty much the same. Follow in their footsteps with this chapter, from their decision to leave through the voyage and the processing at Ellis Island.

MIGRATION FACTORS

While people have many reasons—most of them rooted in economics—to leave one country and resettle in another, British social scientist E.G. Ravenstein identified "The Laws of Migration" in his essay of the same name published in 1889 in the *Journal of the Royal Statistical Society* Vol. 52, No. 2 (June 1889), 241–305. These laws, or factors, include push, pull, and means.

1. *Push Factors*—Elements in the homeland push people to leave, such as religious persecution, economic hardship, mandatory military conscription, etc. "Push" migrants tend to be negatively motivated. They may not want to leave but feel forced to because of unfavorable conditions.

2. *Pull Factors*—Life in the homeland is bearable, but people want something better. Elements in the receiving country pull them in, such as

For More Info

For more on immigration history and migration factors, see Roger Daniels, *Coming to America: A History of Immigration and Ethnicity in American Life* (New York: Perennial, 2002); John Bodnar, *The Transplanted: A History of Immigrants in Urban America* (Bloomington: Indiana University Press, 1985); and Thomas Sowell, *Ethnic America: A History* (New York: Basic Books, 1981).

availability of land, jobs, freedom from religious persecution, etc. These people are positively motivated.

3. *Means*—One must have the ability, the freedom, and the physical and monetary means to migrate. Shifts in transportation technology—from sailing ships to steamships, for example, or cheaper passage—inspired great leaps in immigration statistics.

CHAIN MIGRATION

The United States experienced many notable waves of arrivals—the 1840s–1860s for Irish famine victims, for example, and the 1880s–1920s for eastern and southern Europeans. Immigration naturally declined during wartime and depressions. Whether immigrants arrived as whole family groups or as a few individuals traveling from the homeland together, historians and genealogists have documented a "chain migration," where earlier arrivals sent letters and money home to friends and family, encouraging them to come to America. By linking the chain, you may find relatives you didn't know about.

RETURN AND SEASONAL MIGRATION

During the age of sailing ships, when crossing the Atlantic was a long and dangerous undertaking, most emigrants from Europe never expected to (and never did) see their homeland again. The age of steam, however, changed the way people viewed migration to America. Though many of the arrivals in America planned to settle here, many others came temporarily to work and save money, with the goal of returning to the homeland. Travel by steamship, beginning in the 1850s, made seasonal migration possible, since travel time was reduced greatly. These migrants would leave America after the fall harvest and return to Europe in time for spring planting. English house painters, for example, came to America in the spring, then traveled to Scotland in the summer, and back to England in the fall and winter.

The three groups least likely to return to their homeland were Jews, Irish, and Germans, mainly because they typically arrived as families. **Italians, Poles, and Greeks, however, whose male population migrated first, were more likely to return because their intention was to earn money either to buy land in their native country or to send for their families.** They became known as "birds of passage."

When you find your ancestor on a passenger list or index, always look for additional entries that may follow or precede by a couple of years, especially if the ancestor was Italian, Polish, or Greek. Albino DeBartolo, an Italian immigrant, was a typical bird of passage. Albino first came to America in 1905; he went back to Italy around 1907–1908; he came back to America in 1909; he went back to Italy about 1911; then he made his final return to America in 1912.

Notes

AMERICAN IMMIGRATION HISTORY BY TIME PERIODS

Immigration to America has been constant, but the number of immigrants has ebbed and flowed over the centuries. Historians have conveniently divided American immigration history into these major time periods:

I. Colonial Period (late 1500s–1776)

Main Groups: Spanish, French, English, African, Dutch, German, Welsh, Finnish, Scottish, Scotch-Irish

II. 1776–1820

Main Groups: Continuation of same groups as Colonial period, but in decreasing numbers. Due to international wars and early attempts at immigration restriction, immigration to America grew only slightly during this period.

III. 1820–ca. 1880

Main Groups: Catholic Irish, Norwegian, Swedish, Danish, German, Chinese, Japanese, French Canadian.

IV. ca. 1880–ca. 1920

Main Groups: Italian, Polish, Austrian, Czech, Slovak, Yugoslav, Romanian, Russian, Hungarian, Armenian, Greek, Arabic, Jewish, Japanese.

V. ca. 1920–1945

Main Groups: German, Italian, Polish, Czech (esp. 1921–1930); British (English, Scottish, Welsh) and Irish; Canadian and Mexican; and refugees from Nazi Germany. Immigration to America declined, beginning in 1915, because of U.S. legislation that restricted immigration through quota systems and literacy tests. Migration to and from the homeland was most common during the 1920s. The Great Depression and World War II limited immigration further.

VI. Post–World War II

Main Groups: Mexican, Central and South American, Caribbean, Korean, Vietnamese, Laotian, Cambodian, Middle Eastern Arab, and Soviet Jewish. Because of World War II and the Cold War, the United States accepted European displaced persons and refugees (for example, German, Italian, and Hungarian) during this period. Note: During most periods, immigration from Canada was high and included many British and other European migrants.

THE VOYAGE

Most immigrants coming to America during the Ellis Island years traveled third class in steerage, and their shipboard experience and processing procedures through Ellis Island were fairly common. A one-way steerage ticket cost about

$35 at that time. This was the equivalent of several months—if not years—of savings for many newcomers. After acquiring identity papers and a passport, emigrants traveled to the nearest port city and stayed in a tiny, mock village set up by the steamship company. Here, they were given antiseptic baths and quarantined for five days in a "pest house" as a precaution against contagious diseases. The men were given short haircuts, and both men and women had their scalps washed with a soft soap, carbolic acid (a disinfectant), and petroleum. Since the steamship companies had to absorb the cost of return passage for anyone who did not pass the health inspections in America, the emigrants were given medical examinations and vaccinations before departure.[1]

After a stay at the pest house for at least five days, the waiting passengers were then taken through the streets to the docks. Steamship representatives compiled the ship's manifest, or list of passengers. They recorded such information as name, age, sex, occupation, and marital status; last residence; final destination in the United States; if ever in the United States before—when, where, and for how long; if going to join a relative, the relative's name, address, and relationship; whether able to read and write; whether in possession of a train ticket to the final destination; who paid the passage; amount of money the passenger was carrying; whether the passenger was a polygamist or had ever been in prison, almshouse, or institution for the insane; the passenger's state of health; a personal description that included height, complexion, color of hair and eyes, and identifying marks; place of birth; and name and address of closest living relative in native country.[2]

While most of the steamships were capable of carrying about fifteen hundred third-class passengers, steerage was typically overcrowded with several hundred more than capacity. The steerage compartment, so named because it was located below deck, where the steering mechanism was, contained little ventilation. The floors were wooden and sprinkled with sand to absorb spills or dampness. Although they were swept daily, they were not washed during the two-week voyage.[3]

The large steerage compartment contained tiers of bunks. Each iron berth had a straw mattress covered by a slip of white canvas. The bunk had no pillow; substituted in its place was each passenger's life jacket. A short, light-weight blanket was also provided and became part of the emigrant's possessions. To the travelers, the berth became their space, serving as a bed, clothes and towel rack, and baggage storage area.[4]

No real provisions were made for the passengers to be clean. Most ships had no hooks for clothes, no trash containers, and no cans for seasickness. No wonder passengers had a reputation for being filthy; they had no choice.[5]

Each passenger was supplied with eating utensils, usually a fork, spoon, and tin lunch pail. A typical breakfast might consist of coffee and a biscuit. For dinner, passengers ate soup and one dish without meat every two days, and one dish with meat every five days. For supper, they would be fed one dish with

Notes

Endnotes begin on page 95.

meat, wine, and bread. After meals, the passengers washed their own dishes, using their own soap and towels. Sometimes the steerage area might have only one faucet of warm water. With more than fifteen hundred people waiting to use it, some may have opted to get the grease off their tins with cold salt water.[6]

Many steamships generally had only two washrooms, and these were used by both men and women at the same time. The washrooms contained small basins that the passengers used as a dish tub for their greasy tins, as a laundry tub for their clothing, and as a receptacle to bathe their bodies. These basins received no special cleaning between uses, and they were the only containers to be found for seasickness.[7]

The passengers were supposed to undergo daily medical examinations during the voyage; however, they usually received but two—one at the beginning of the voyage and one toward the end. Lined up in single file, a ship's doctor casually glanced over the travelers while an assistant would punch several holes at a time in a health inspection card. One punch was to represent each of the supposed daily exams.[8] As one passenger recalled, they

> lived for two weeks in disorder and in surroundings that offended every
> sense. Only the fresh breeze from the sea overcame the sickening odors.
> The vile language of the men, the screams of the women defending them-

selves, the crying of the children . . . practically every sound that reached the ear irritated beyond endurance. . . . Everything was dirty, sticky, and disagreeable to the touch. . . . Worse than this was the general air of immorality. . . . All around [was] improper, indecent, and forced mingling of men and women who were total strangers and often did not understand one word of the same language.[9]

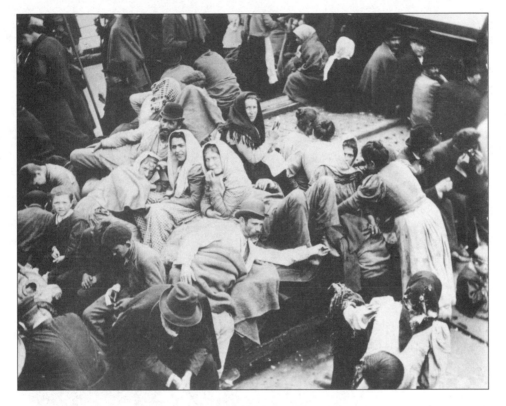

Figure 7-2
Photo courtesy of the Ellis Island Immigration Museum.

On rougher voyages the decks would reek of vomit. Since bad weather prevented them from using the small, open deck allotted to them during the voyage, the immigrants spent day and night in their berths, "listening to the sick moan and groan." Besides the stench of unwashed bodies and vomit, travelers endured vermin such as rats, roaches, and lice. For those who did not survive the voyage, a burial at sea was common.[10]

Burials at sea occurred when someone died aboard ship with too much time remaining between the death and arrival in America to keep the body from decomposing. In rare cases, a body might be preserved in alcohol until the ship reached its arrival port. Those who were buried at sea were wrapped in a canvas shroud with weights attached to the body to keep it from floating to the surface. One can only imagine the heartache of having to watch as a loved one was sent overboard.

No wonder emigrants would "arrive at the journey's end with a mind unfit for healthy, wholesome impressions and with a body weakened and unfit for the hardships that were involved in the beginning of life in the new land."[11]

When the weather was nice, however, the immigrants could wander along their allotted deck. Although the first- and second-class passengers were provided with entertainment, the third-class passengers had to provide their own. Singing and dancing were a common diversion to the otherwise daily monotony of steamship travel in the early twentieth century.[12]

ARRIVAL

After two weeks of these poor conditions, ships heading for the Port of New York passed through a narrow waterway between Brooklyn and Staten Island. Getting their first glimpse of America, the newcomers no doubt focused on the Statue of Liberty that had been unveiled in New York Harbor on October 28, 1886. The passengers' faces were "lit up with hope and fear, joy and sorrow. Hope for success in the new land; . . . fear of the unknown future; joy that the long-dreaded voyage is over; and sorrow at the memories tugging" at their hearts.[13]

Figure 7-3
Photo courtesy of the Ellis Island Immigration Museum.

A small cutter approached the ship from which a U.S. doctor boarded and checked everyone for obvious signs of illness. He also checked with the ship's doctor for any contagious diseases. If there were none, then the ship came to port at a wharf. This was where the first- and second-class passengers were docked. The third class, however, was loaded onto ferry barges and taken to Ellis Island.[14]

A TIMELINE OF ELLIS ISLAND HISTORY

Long before Annie Moore stepped foot on Ellis Island as the first immigrant to be processed there on 2 January 1892, the island had a unique history. The Delaware Indians (Lenni Lenape tribe) called the island *Kioshk* or Gull Island, but when the Dutch settled New York and discovered oyster fishing to be plentiful off the island, they renamed it Oyster Island. Here's a historical timeline of Ellis Island:

1661	Dutch name is Oyster Island.
1674–1680	Governor Andross grants the island to Captain William Dyre.
1686	William and Mary Dyre sell the island to Thomas and Patience Lloyd.
1696	Thomas Lloyd dies and the island is sold to pay off his debts; identity of owners is unknown until Samuel Ellis buys the property. The date he purchases it is unknown.
1765	Island is known as Gibbet Island, and it becomes a site for the execution of pirates.
1778	Samuel Ellis is owner of the island by November 18.
1785	Ellis puts the island up for sale.
1794	Samuel Ellis dies. In his will he bequeaths the island to the unborn child of his pregnant daughter, Catherine Westervelt, "should it be a son. . . . Should it prove to be a daughter, then in that case she comes, with the rest of the children, for an equal proportion" of the island. Samuel also requests that the boy be given his name. Although Catherine gives birth to a son, he dies in infancy. Family members then dispute the title to the island, but it passes into the hands of Samuel's two remaining daughters, Elizabeth Ellis Ryerson and Rachel Ellis Cooder.
1798	Ellis Island serves as a military enlisting headquarters. Although still in private hands, the island is made into a fort from fear of attacks from the British.
1808	New York buys Ellis Island and is immediately reimbursed by the federal government, who takes possession of the island. Fort Gibson is built on the island just before the outbreak of the War of 1812. The fort is never needed.
1861	Fort Gibson is dismantled, and the island is used to store ammunition.

Continued on next page

1890   Castle Garden facilities are deemed inadequate to handle influx of immigrants, so Ellis Island is chosen as the site to replace it. Landfill, from excavations for New York's subway system and Grand Central Station, is used to double the size of the island. The first buildings are made from Georgia pine. Some of the old Fort Gibson brick buildings are used as dormitories.

1892   The new immigrant receiving station opens on January 1, with fifteen-year-old Annie Moore from County Cork, Ireland, being the first person admitted. She receives a $10 gold piece.

1897   Fire breaks out on the island on the night of June 14/morning of June 15. No life is lost, but the buildings are destroyed. Inspections are moved to the Barge Office at Battery Park.

1900   On 17 December, Ellis Island reopens with buildings made from brick.

1907   On 17 April, an all-time record of arrivals embark at Ellis Island: 11,747, with more than a million arriving in that one year.

1914   World War I begins and immigration to the United States is halted.

1917   Ellis Island operates as a military installation and hospital.

1921   Quota laws are passed, reducing the number of immigrants.

1924   Quota laws are revised, further reducing the number of immigrants, and the buildings on Ellis Island are victims of neglect and abandonment.

1954–   Ellis Island is placed under the jurisdiction of the General Services Ad-
1964   ministration, and all buildings are officially closed in November 1954.

1965   Ellis Island falls under the jurisdiction of the National Park Service as part of the Statue of Liberty National Monument.

1976   Ellis Island opens to the public.

1984   Restoration begins on Ellis Island.

1990   Ellis Island reopens to the public as a museum.

Source: *Ellis Island*, an undated, unpublished manuscript prepared by the New York City Writers' Project, Works Projects Administration; III-NNE-112: Records Pertaining to the History of Ellis Island (from Private Papers of Ione G. Lemmon); National Archives Gift Collection, Record Group 316; National Archives at College Park–Archives II. (Ref. Finding Aid NC-42, Entry # 63.) See also the chronology in Barry Moreno's *Encyclopedia of Ellis Island*.

As with the ship, the barge was overcrowded, crammed with nine hundred people but built for six hundred. This might have been acceptable for the short trip down the river, but each barge usually had to wait hours to disembark its passengers—and it contained hardly any toilet facilities.[15]

ELLIS ISLAND

The original building on Ellis Island was made of Georgia pine and spruce. Unfortunately, five years after the island opened as an immigrant receiving station, a fire broke out shortly after midnight on 15 June 1897. About two hundred immigrants, most Italian, were on the island at the time, some in the hospital but most in the dormitories. All were safely evacuated. Initially after the fire, immigrants received inspections on the piers where the vessel docked. Those passing the exams were released, those who were sick were sent to New York City hospitals, and those with contagious diseases were put in quarantine. Anyone who was detained was lodged in the barge office at Battery Park.[16]

During the two and a half years it took to construct the new building, inspections took place at the barge office. The new brick building opened on 17 December 1900.[17] As the immigrants disembarked from the ferry boat, they were tagged with a number that corresponded to their number-placement on the ship's passenger list. As a group they were led into the main building, where their baggage was inspected. They were then led up a stairway where, unbeknownst to them, the first of a series of medical inspections took place. Inspectors were stationed at various points along the stairway and watched arrivals for obvious signs of physical defects, derangements, and heart and lung problems. Inspectors stopped immigrants with potential problems and marked their dark clothing on the front shoulder with chalk, such as with an *H* for heart problems.[18]

At the first station in the huge Registry Hall, a surgeon checked each arrival's health inspection card from aboard ship. Immigrants were most likely

FIRE ON ELLIS ISLAND

It Broke Out Shortly After Midnight in the Furnace of the Main Building.

THE FIREBOAT NEW YORKER AND POLICE BOAT PATROL HAVE GONE TO THE SCENE.

Communication With Island Was Cut Off—It Was Reported that All Persons Escaped With Their Lives.

Fire broke out in the main building of the United States Immigration Station, on Ellis Island, shortly after midnight. It was first discovered from this city, when the flames began to shoot out from the northwest tower. This was at 12:30.

Figure 7-5
New York Times, 15 June 1897, page 1.

Figure 7-4
Original building on Ellis Island made of Georgia pine. Photo courtesy of the Ellis Island Immigration Museum.

Figure 7-6
Main building on Ellis Island, which opened 17 December 1900. Photo courtesy of the Ellis Island Immigration Museum.

Figure 7-7
Immigrants arriving on Ellis Island. Photo courtesy of the Ellis Island Immigration Museum.

prepared for the second station's exam. Even before many had left their home-lands, they were warned by earlier travelers to "beware of the eye man." He was checking for trachoma, a highly contagious eye disease that caused blindness. Anyone found to have it was immediately deported.[19]

After completing the medical exams, the newcomers were instructed to sit in a waiting pen where each manifest group had its own area. While they waited, they heard the sounds of mingling languages, crying children, and yelling guards.[20]

See Also

For more on the medical exams, see chapter eight.

QUESTIONING

A registry clerk called up one manifest group at a time. These clerks, dressed in military-style uniforms, frightened many of the immigrants. Some had left their homeland to avoid military conscription. Now the first person they had to deal with reeked of this type of authority.[21]

With hundreds of interpreters to help, the clerk, "armed with a copy of the manifest sheet," would ask immigrants the same questions as on the manifest sheet and compare the answers. If any discrepancies were found, he could have the new arrival detained. Two of the most troublesome questions for immigrants were "Do you have a job waiting?" and "Who paid your passage?" In 1885, the U.S. government had outlawed labor contracts, but many contractors simply went underground. Once on Ellis Island, if the new arrival had no job waiting, the immigrant had to convince the clerk that he was not likely to become a public charge.[22]

The arrivals were never told the results of any of the exams. They were simply pushed forward into another waiting area until their names were called so that they might leave the island.[23]

Women had a slightly different immigration experience than men. Many of the women who arrived during the peak years came alone or with small children. Typically, most of the women who immigrated were young and healthy, and they may have been married only a few months or perhaps a couple of years before their husbands embarked for America. Their husbands

Figure 7-8
Tagged immigrant family. The tag gave their names and their placement on the passenger arrival list. Photo courtesy of the Ellis Island Immigration Museum.

Figure 7-9
Penned areas where immigrants waited for inspections. Photo courtesy of the Ellis Island Immigration Museum.

had come to America first, working to save enough money to pay for their wives' and children's passage. Once the passage money arrived, each woman had the responsibility of selling furniture and possessions that could not be carried aboard ship. She had to obtain the necessary traveling documents and steamship tickets, then find a way to get to the port city. Most women had never gone beyond the borders of their native villages before. Certainly, they had never experienced dealing with bureaucrats. Some women—married and single—were forced to submit to a demand for sexual favors before they were given the papers they needed to emigrate.[24]

Once they reached America and Ellis Island, unescorted women were detained until someone arrived to pick them up. The U.S. government did not want to encourage prostitution or the white slave trade, so if a male claiming to be a woman's fiancé arrived to claim her, the couple might be married or contracted to marry right there on Ellis Island.[25]

Figure 7-10
Receiving room on Ellis Island, showing the route immigrants took in their processing. Photo courtesy of the Ellis Island Immigration Museum.

RECEIVING ROOM AT ELLIS ISLAND

(A) Entrance stairs; (B) Examination of health ticket; (C) Surgeon's examination; (D) Second surgeon's examination; (E) Group compartments; (F) Waiting for inspection; (G) Passage to the stairway; (H) Detention room; (I) The Inspectors' desks; (K) Outward passage to barge, ferry, or detention room.

DETENTION

Inspectors were told to detain idiots, imbeciles, epileptics, the feebleminded, the senile, and the insane. Characteristics they watched for were talkativeness, being a smart aleck, eroticism or flirtatiousness, boisterousness, surliness, intoxication, confusion and disorientation, aimlessness, stuttering, and excessive friendliness.[26]

Those who were detained had nothing to do except sit on hard wooden benches. The men and women were generally kept separated, but occasional

Figure 7-11
Registry clerk desk where immigrants were called up for questioning. The clerk was armed with a copy of the passenger arrival list (manifest) and asked the immigrant the same questions asked at the port of departure. If there were any discrepancies, the immigrant could be detained. Photo courtesy of the Ellis Island Immigration Museum.

visits to the roof garden allowed mingling and a time for children to run around a small playground. Representatives from immigrant aid and other societies, such as the Society for the Protection of Italian Immigrants, the Daughters of the American Revolution (DAR), and the Young Men's Christian Association (YMCA), helped occupy the immigrants, teaching them English and how to be "good" Americans.[27]

For a time, men and women ate in separate dining halls, where detainees were sometimes fed without forks, spoons, or knives. If there happened to be an insufficient number of bowls or plates, they were likely to be reused, without washing, until everyone had been fed.[28]

A typical 1906 menu was as follows:

Breakfast	Coffee with milk and sugar
	Bread and butter
	Crackers and milk for women and children

Dinner	Beef stew, boiled potatoes, and rye bread
	Smoked or pickled herring for Hebrews
	Crackers and milk for women and children
Supper	Baked beans, stewed prunes, and rye bread
	Tea with milk and sugar
	Crackers and milk for women and children

One delicacy served on Ellis Island was prune sandwiches. Ellis Island ordered twenty million prunes a year. By 1905, they were served only twice weekly. This was not because the treat was becoming monotonous, but because, as one waiter described it, the floor was like a skating rink from all the discarded slimy prune pits. In the dining rooms, many immigrants ate their first banana—peel and all.[29]

Figure 7-13
Multi-language U.S. citizenship manuals published by the National Society, Daughters of the American Revolution and distributed at Ellis Island between 1921 and the early 1950s. The DAR had a room on Ellis Island connected to the detention corridor by a window. Immigrants called the window the "window of hope" where the DAR ladies handed out yarn, fabric, and thread to the detained women. To get more materials, immigrant women had to show a completed piece. One immigrant woman allegedly said, "Here comes the Revolutionary Lady. Now we will have something to do." Photo taken by the author; manuals courtesy of the National Society, Daughters of the American Revolution, Americana Collection.

Figure 7-14
Dining hall on Ellis Island. Photo courtesy of the Ellis Island Immigration Museum.

DEPORTATION

As early as 1893, the Supreme Court had ruled that incoming migrants did not have a right to land and had no right to a legal hearing if authoritites decided to deport them. During the Board of Special Inquiry held on Ellis Island, newcomers were not allowed to confer with relatives or an attorney unless they were given an unfavorable decision to be deported.[30]

About one thousand people each month were considered "undesirable." This was why the immigrants referred to the receiving station as the Island of Hope, Island of Tears. Being diseased or likely to be a public charge was cause for immediate deportation. By 1909, if the immigrant did not have at least $25 cash in his possession, he was deported.[31]

Returning to their homeland meant disgrace. All their hopes and dreams were lost. They had sold all their possessions to pay for their passage. Agonizing decisions had to be made when one member of the family was not admitted. The heartbreaking question became, do they say good-bye to their family member or return to their homeland together?[32]

Henry Curran, a commissioner of Ellis Island, wrote about the deportees in 1923:

> Day by day the barges took them from Ellis Island back to the ships again, back to the ocean, back to—what? As they trooped aboard the big barges under my window, carrying their heavy bundles, some in their colorful native costumes worn to celebrate their first glad day in free America, some carrying little American flags, most of them quietly weeping, they twisted something in my heart.[33]

A morgue and crematory were installed on Ellis Island, and several immi-

Figure 7-15
The Board of Special Inquiry. Photo courtesy of the Ellis Island Immigration Museum.

grants committed suicide during its history. Others who were rejected took their lives by jumping overboard on the voyage back.[34]

Those who passed the inspections also had to deal with bribery, cheating, and petty thievery by other immigrants and by Ellis Island personnel. Although each new commissioner embarked upon a plan to "clean matters up," these conditions often continued.[35]

Figure 7-16
Photo courtesy of the Ellis Island Immigration Museum.

A NEW LIFE

Once the immigrants' names were read and they were allowed to leave, they were taken to the money exchange office to trade their foreign currency and were then escorted to the ferries that would take them to transportation and their final destinations.[36]

The next hurdle they would encounter was living in America. "Everything, human contact, work, language, living quarters, climate, and food becomes a problem to be resolved, a difficulty to overcome. They suddenly realize that they know nothing anymore." They must begin again.[37]

Unlike the transplanted of the seventeenth and early eighteenth centuries who were called "colonists" and "settlers," these newcomers were labeled "immigrants." They now coped with prejudices and stereotypes that they would find bewildering and humiliating.[38] But through all these obstacles most stayed and settled in America, making a new and better life for themselves and their families.

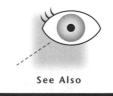

See Also

Full citations can be found in the Bibliography, pages 153–158.

ENDNOTES

[1] Oxford, "Hope, Tears, and Remembrance," 36; Dunne and Tifft, *Ellis Island*, n.p.; Shapiro, *Gateway to Liberty*, 77, 85-87; Price, "What I Learned by Traveling from Naples to New York in the Steerage," 3-5, 14.

[2] Shapiro, *Gateway to Liberty*, 78; Colletta, *They Came in Ships*, 36-37.

[3] Shapiro, *Gateway to Liberty*, 78.

[4] Abbott, *Immigration: Select Documents and Case Records*, 82-86.

[5] Abbott, *Immigration: Select Documents and Case Records*, 82-86.

[6] Abbott, *Immigration: Select Documents and Case Records*, 82-86.

[7] Abbott, *Immigration: Select Documents and Case Records*, 82-86.

[8] Abbott, *Immigration: Select Documents and Case Records*, 82-86.

[9] Abbott, *Immigration: Select Documents and Case Records*, 86.

[10] Quote from interview with Fred Ebetino, 1990; DeConde, *Half Bitter, Half Sweet: An Excursion into Italian-American History*, 71; Marshall, "Makes Six Ocean Trips to Study Steerage Reform" SM10; Oxford, "Hope, Tears, and Remembrance," 40.

[11] Bolino, *The Ellis Island Source Book*, 13.

[12] Marshall, "Makes Six Ocean Trips to Study Steerage Reform," SM10.

[13] Bolino, *The Ellis Island Source Book*, 14-15; quote from Oxford, "Hope, Tears, and Remembrance," 42.

[14] Bolino, *The Ellis Island Source Book*, 14-15; Shapiro, *Gateway to Liberty*, 121.

[15] Shapiro, *Gateway to Liberty*, 155.

[16] "Fire on Ellis Island," p. 1; "Caring for Immigrants," p. 1; "Immigrants on the Piers," p. 12.

[17] Shapiro, *Gateway to Liberty*, 130-131, 138.

[18] Bolino, *The Ellis Island Source Book*, 14-15; Shapiro, *Gateway to Liberty*, 160; Pitkin, *Keepers of the Gate*, 68-69.

[19] Bolino, *The Ellis Island Source Book*, 14-15; Pitkin, *Keepers of the Gate*, 68-69; Shapiro, *Gateway to Liberty*, 159-160; quote from Oxford, "Hope, Tears, and Remembrance," 42.

[20] Shapiro, *Gateway to Liberty*, 165; Bolino, *The Ellis Island Source Book*, 17.

[21] Shapiro, *Gateway to Liberty*, 165; Chermayeff, *Ellis Island*, 119.

[22] First quote, Pitkin, *Keepers of the Gate*, 22-23; quoted questions, Giordano, *The Italian American Catalog*, 203; Bass, "A New Life Begins for the Island of Hope and Tears," 90.

[23] Oxford, "Hope, Tears, and Remembrance," 68-70.

[24] Mangione and Morreale, *La Storia*, 92-94.

[25] Bolino, *The Ellis Island Source Book*, 18, 20.

[26] Bolino, *The Ellis Island Source Book*, 3.

[27] Shapiro, *Gateway to Liberty*, 153, 217-218; Speranza, "How It Feels to Be a Problem," 457-463.

[28] Shapiro, *Gateway to Liberty*, 142-143.

[29] Chermayeff, *Ellis Island*, 154; Shapiro, *Gateway to Liberty*, 144; Hall, "New Life for Ellis Island," 95.

[30] Bolino, *The Ellis Island Source Book*, 21, 25.

[31] Shapiro, *Gateway to Liberty*, 199; Oxford, "Hope, Tears, and Remembrance," 69.

[32] Shapiro, *Gateway to Liberty*, 210.

[33] Oxford, "Hope, Tears, and Remembrance," 69.

[34] Dunne and Tifft, *Ellis Island*, n.p.

[35] Shapiro, *Gateway to Liberty*, 138-139.

[36] *Island of Hope, Island of Tears*, video.

[37] Quote from Cerase, "Expectations and Reality," 245-262.

[38] Daniels, *Coming to America*, 29; Cerase, "Expectations and Reality," 245.

CHAPTER 8

Ellis Island Medical Records

W hen Emma Lazarus penned the famous lines in her sonnet "The New Colossus," "Give me your tired, your poor, your huddled masses yearning to breathe free," she did not include "your sick and diseased." Before immigrants left their homeland, the steamship companies were supposed to vaccinate, disinfect, and determine the health of their passengers prior to departure. The medical exams were typically superficial, however. Once the ship arrived at New York, a physician for the U.S. Marine Hospital Service[1] boarded the ship and gave quick medical exams to the first- and second-class passengers in the privacy of their cabins. After a cursory inspection of the third-, or steerage-class passengers to make sure they'd suffered no outbreaks of cholera, smallpox, typhus, or yellow fever, the passengers boarded a barge that took them to Ellis Island. Ships carrying passengers with contagious diseases, however, were quarantined and flew a yellow flag at their masthead. Those passengers were taken to one of the other islands in New York Harbor.

QUARANTINED PASSENGERS

People en route to Ellis Island who were sick with a contagious disease aboard ship were subsequently taken to hospitals on Hoffman and Swinburne (formerly Dix) islands. Both islands were created from dredged sand in New York Harbor in the 1860s and opened as quarantine stations in the early 1870s. The hospitals on these islands were in operation until the late 1920s.

If passengers were suffering from a contagious disease upon arrival, they were sent to Swinburne Island; if they were just exposed to a contagious disease but not showing symptoms, they were sent to Hoffman Island for observation during the incubation period of the disease. Once cleared from either of these two islands, arrivals then went on to Castle Garden or Ellis Island, depending on the year of arrival.

Notes

Endnotes for this chapter begin on page 107.

For More Info

For more on the various islands used for sick and quarantined passengers, see Sharon Seitz and Stuart Miller's *The Other Islands of New York City* (Woodstock, Vt.: The Countryman Press, 2001).

Reminder

For More Info

A fascinating book on immigrants and disease is Alan M. Kraut's *Silent Travelers: Germs, Genes, and the "Immigrant Menace."* (New York: Basic Books, 1994).

During the 1892 cholera epidemic, about fifteen ships a day arrived in New York. If your ancestors arrived in that year, **you'll want to check for the ship's name in *The New York Times* (see chapter nine) to see if it was diverted to one of the other islands for quarantine.**

"The Forgotten of Ellis Island: Deaths in Quarantine, 1909–1911" <http://freepages.genealogy.rootsweb.com/~quarantine/index.htm> is a helpful Web site managed by Cathy Horn, which lists names and information for 418 individuals, 85 percent of whom were children under age thirteen. She also has compiled an extensive bibliography of books and articles about immigrants and quarantine, as well as links to other sites.

Also helpful for learning more about the Hoffman-Swinburne records is Rafael Guber's article, "When Genealogists Read History, Part 2" <www.ancestry.com/library/view/ancmag/847.asp>, which goes into further detail. According to Guber's article, "Passengers with 'In Hospital' next to their names [on passenger lists] might never have made it to Ellis Island. . . . It appears that Hoffman and Swinburne islands formed the first line of defense against airborne diseases," such as yellow fever, typhus, smallpox, and so forth.

IF THEY MADE IT TO ELLIS ISLAND

As mentioned in the previous chapter, officials tagged immigrants upon landing with a number that corresponded to their number on the ship's passenger list. As a group, they were led into the main building, where their baggage was inspected. Immigrants were then instructed to walk up a stairway where, unbeknownst to them, the first of a series of medical inspections took place. Public Health Service doctors were stationed at various points along the stairway and watched arrivals as they climbed the stairs, looking for obvious signs of health problems, such as wheezing, coughing, limping, or shortness of breath. The inspectors asked children their names to make sure they weren't deaf or dumb. For those immigrants with potential problems, the doctors marked their dark clothing on the front shoulder with chalk, such as an *H* for heart problems.[2]

At the first station in the huge Registry Hall, an inspector checked each arrival's health inspection card from aboard ship. After stamping it, he handed it back to the immigrant and watched. The unsuspecting person would look to see what the inspector had stamped on the card and would inadvertently reveal any eye problems. Immigrants who held the card too close to their eyes for viewing or too far away tipped off inspectors.[3]

Immigrants were most likely prepared for the second station's exam. Even before many had left their homeland, they were warned by earlier travelers to "beware of the eye man." Each was checked for trachoma, a highly contagious eye disease that causes blindness.[4] "To turn the eyelid, I used the good old buttoner," stated Dr. Grover Kempf, a U.S. Public Health physician at

Ellis Island. "This was a little loop [used] to button shoes; [we] used [it] to turn the eyelid. It was the most efficient way of turning the eyes ever devised."[5] Prior to 1905, physicians examined only those immigrants who exhibited symptoms. After this date, all immigrants' eyelids were everted. Between exams physicians dipped the hook into a disinfecting solution. As one might imagine, this exam was greatly feared and quite painful. Any immigrant who had trachoma was immediately deported.[6]

Figure 8-1
Inspectors performing eye exam. Photo courtesy of the Ellis Island Immigration Museum.

If health inspectors noted any problems during these line exams, they indicated the diagnosis on the immigrant's clothing in chalk: *C* for conjunctivitis, *Ct* for trachoma, *Ft* for feet problems, *Pg* for pregnant, *K* for hernia, and *X* for possible mental retardation. Inspectors were told to detain idiots, imbeciles, epileptics, the feebleminded, the senile, and the insane. Characteristics they watched for were talkativeness, being a smart aleck, eroticism or flirtatiousness, boisterousness, surliness, intoxication, confusion and disorientation, aimlessness, stuttering, and excessive friendliness. Marked immigrants were taken out of line and given more thorough examinations.[7]

The sexes were segregated for these medical exams, and women physicians and nurses examined women immigrants. By 1924, the Public Health Service had four female physicians on duty. Yet most immigrant women found the exams embarrassing and traumatizing. Even though the exam was done by women, the children were all there, and most women had to strip to the waist.

Figure 8-2
Woman with chalk lettering on her left shoulder. Photo courtesy of the Ellis Island Immigration Museum.

Figure 8-3
Men's medical examination. Photo courtesy of the Ellis Island Immigration Museum.

After completing the medical exams, the newcomers were instructed to sit in a waiting pen where each manifest group had its own area. The arrivals were never told the results of any of the exams. They were simply herded into another waiting area until their names were called so that they might leave, or they might be taken to other facilities on the island.

Figure 8-4
Buildings opposite main building. The building to the left was the administration building; the one to the right was the first hospital built on Ellis Island. Photo courtesy of the Ellis Island Immigration Museum.

Ellis Island had its own hospital, contagious disease ward, mental ward, autopsy theater, morgue, and crematory. The hospital on Ellis Island opened in 1902; prior to that time, "federal officials contracted hospital services from the New York City Health Department and the Long Island College Hospital in Brooklyn, among others." By 1911, more than fifteen buildings on Ellis Island were devoted to medical care. That same year, physicians examined nearly 750,000 immigrants. Of these, almost 17,000 had physical or mental defects, which included 1,363 who had loathsome or dangerous contagious diseases and 1,167 who had trachoma. Dangerous contagious diseases included trachoma and pulmonary tuberculosis. Loathsome diseases included favus (scalp and nail fungus), syphilis, gonorrhea, and leprosy. Those who were detained for observation or recuperation underwent daily delousing, where immigrants were stripped naked to have their clothing fumigated. During the Island's history, more than 3,500 immigrants died on the Island, including some 1,400 children, and more than 350 babies were born.[8]

MEDICAL RECORDS

If your ancestor was detained on Ellis Island for medical or other reasons, you have an additional resource to explore: Beginning about 1903, the passenger arrival lists included a supplemental section for detainees, known as the Record of Detained

Important

Aliens. Surviving lists were microfilmed with their corresponding passenger lists at the end of the lists of arrivals. They contain the name of each detainee, the cause for the detention, and the date and time of discharge. The abbreviation *LCD* meant "loathsome [or] contagious disease."

Deported immigrants will be listed following the Record of Detained Aliens on the Record of Aliens Held for Special Inquiry. (You'll find a notation by the immigrant's name on the passenger list: "S.I.") On this form, the cause of the detention or rejection was noted, as were actions taken by the Board of Special Inquiry, the date of hearings, the number of meals eaten during detention, and if deported, the date, name of vessel, and port from which they returned to their native land. Be sure to check subsequent passenger lists and indexes for aliens who were deported for medical reasons, but may have reentered the country at a future date when they might have been able to pass inspection or come via first- or second-class where the exams weren't as rigid.

If you have a relative who was born or died on Ellis Island, the event should be recorded among the New York City (Manhattan) birth and death records. The death record should tell you if the relative was cremated on the island, or if the body was removed for burial and where interment took place.

As for admittance and discharge registers associated with the hospital and medical facilities on Ellis Island, or on Hoffman or Swinburne islands, some

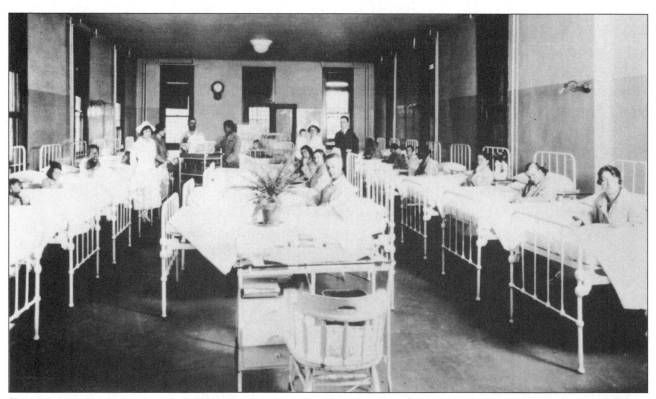

Figure 8-5
Hospital ward. Photo courtesy of the Ellis Island Immigration Museum.

of these records are preserved on microfilm and in the custody of the U.S. Department of Health and Human Services, National Hansen's Disease Programs, in Baton Rouge, Louisiana <www.hrsa.gov>. According to the staff there, the records are not indexed, and they are unable to assist researchers in locating records on immigrant ancestors.[9]

Scattered among National Archives Record Group 85, Records of the Immigration and Naturalization Service, entry 9, however, you'll find various documents relating to hospital and medical records on Ellis Island. Unfortunately, this record group has no index and the records have not been microfilmed. You'll need to go to the National Archives in Washington, D.C., to view them. These records generally relate to administrative matters and construction of the hospital buildings, but some files have cases specific to immigrants who were in danger of being deported for a medical reason.

An example is the file of Theodor Kelsch, who arrived on the *Finland* from Antwerp on 10 August 1908 (T715, roll 1128, volume 2477, group 3, list 21). According to the passenger list's Record of Aliens Held for Special Inquiry, sixteen-year-old Theodor was placed in the hospital upon arrival. The file in Record Group 85, entry 9, file #51881-129 tells the story of the threat to deport him because he had trachoma. The file includes a transcript of the Board of Special Inquiry's hearing where Theodor's father appeared on his son's behalf on 13 August 1908. Look at how rich the genealogical information is in this document and the clues and leads to other documents:

> At a meeting of a Board of Special Inquiry held at Ellis Island, N.Y., this 13th day of August, 1908, 11.35 A.M.
>
> PRESENT: Inspectors PARBURY (Chairman), TONER and BROPHY.
>
> Excluded case. SS "Finland," Red Star Line, August 10, 1908. Inspector Jackson.
>
> Taken up on order of Commissioner for the purpose of allowing witness to testify as to citizenship.
>
> WITNESS, called and sworn by Inspector Parbury, testified in English as follows:
>
> BY MR. PARBURY:
>
> > Q. What is your name?   A. Balhaser Kelsch.
> > Q. Where do you live?   A. Bowen St., Westchester, N.Y.
> > Q. For whom do you call?   A. My son.
> > Q. What is his name?   A. Theordor Kelsch.
> > Q. How old is he?   A. Going to be 16 years 18th of September.
> > Q. How long have you been in the United States?   A. Since 16 years.
> > Q. Did you come to the United States after your son was born or before?   A. Before the boy was born.

Q. About how long before?   A. In August I came over to Philadelphia and he was born in September.

Q. Have you ever seen your son?   A. Last Monday on the boat.

Q. That is the only time you have seen him?   A. Yes.

Q. Are you a citizen of the United States?   A. Yes sir (Shows paper issued in Supreme Court, State of New York, First Judicial District, which shows that Balhaser Kelsch was admitted to be a citizen of the United States on the 8 day of November, 1897; signed by Henry D. Purroy, Clerk of the Court.)

Q. Where is your wife?   A. Up in Westchester.

Q. Is she the mother of this son.   A. Yes sir.

Q. How long has she been here?   A. She came a year after me.

Q. Have you children in this country?   A. One child that was born here—a girl.

Q. Who has been supporting this son?   A. My parents.

Q. Have you ever contributed to his support?   A. Sometimes to the parents.

Q. Are your parents still living?   A. Yes sir.

Q. Did you send for this boy?   A. Yes sir.

Q. Pay his passage?   A. Yes sir.

Q. The boy ever been in this country?   A. No.

Q. What is your business?   A. Foreman, Westchester Concrete Block Company.

Q. How much do you earn?   A. $18 a week.

Q. Do you own any property?   A. No sir.

Q. Have you any money saved?   A. No sir; I sent it for my boy to come over.

Q. You understand your boy has been certified by the medical division as having trachoma, and under our laws he cannot land here. Would you desire to make application to have him treated in the hospital here?   A. Yes sir, if it don't cost me too much.

Mr. Toner: I move the former decision [to be excluded] be sustained.

Mr. Brophy: Second the motion.

Mr. Parbury: Former decision sustained.

ALIEN EXCLUDED.

Also in the file are medical certificates and various correspondence, including a handwritten letter dated 9 October 1908 from Theodor's father in German and a typed translation:

Dear sir:

Kindly help a German-American out of an embarrassing situation. My son, Theodor Kelscch, is being detained on Ellis Island on account of

trachoma, and as I am a citizen, I have the right to have him cured here.
I have paid $37.50 and now comes another bill for $51.75. I am not in
a position to pay for all this, having paid his fare as cabin passenger
and his board in Germany. I earn $18 a week, and had saved $300, but
now all my money is gone and I have to look out also for my family
here. I am willing to pay something, but can not possibly raise so much.
It would beggar me. I have always been a good citizen, have never been
arrested, and have been a foreman ever since I came to this country. I
think my son belongs to [sic—with] us, and he will make a good citizen.

Thanking you in advance, and hoping that you will do something for a father of a family,

Respectfully,

B. Kelsch
Westchester, New York City

Theodor was finally admitted to the United States after he recovered and was reunited with his family.

Unfortunately, to find files like this you'll be searching through many folders at the National Archives. Here is a list of those immigrants who came through Ellis Island (other ports were mixed in with these files) found in Record Group 85, entry 9, box 77, files 51881/124–150, for the years 1906–1909. Although all the files for the Ellis Island arrivals were for 1908, surely there were other cases in this one year. Maybe one of these is your ancestor:

File #	Name	Age	Nativity	Ship	Arrival date	Cause
128	Leie Kwarczinsky	30 yrs	Russia	*Bulow*	5 Aug 1908	trachoma
129	Theodor Kelsch	16 yrs	German	*Finland*	10 Aug 1908	trachoma
131	Johan Deutsh	30 yrs	Hungarian-German	*Finland*	10 Aug 1908	tuberculosis
133	Pinelopis Kostantakopoulos	17 yrs	Greece	*Moraitia*	30 July 1908	trachoma
134	Ida Battista	15 yrs	Italy	*Re d'Italia*	13 Aug 1908	trachoma
136	Basse & Srul Silberstein	46 yrs & 9 yrs	Russia	*Bremen*	18 Aug 1908	trachoma
137	Gisella Rosen	16 yrs	Roumania [sic]	*Kronprinzessin Cecilie*	25 Aug 1908	trachoma
141	Itze Krieger	11 yrs	Russia	*Barbarossa*	2 Sept 1908	favus
143	Ruben Blonstein	15 yrs	Russia	*Main*	8 Sept 1908	trachoma
144	Katina & Nickolas Vagopoulon	24 yrs & 12 yrs	Greece	*Moraitis*	30 July 1908	trachoma
145	Masche Kahan	25 yrs	Russia	*Barbarossa*	2 Sept 1908	trachoma
146	Flora Cingoloni	16 yrs	Italy	*Principe di Piemnte*	16 Sept 1908	trachoma
149	Alte Ehrenberg	27 yrs	Russia	*Grosse Kurfurst*	15 Sept 1908	trachoma

The bottom line: Whether your ancestors were tired, poor, or merely yearning to breathe free, the passenger lists are likely your best source to finding out if they were sick, too.

ENDNOTES

1. "The federal physicians charged with health certification of individual new arrivals at immigration depots belonged to the United States Marine Hospital Service [1798–1902], which was renamed the United States Public Health and Marine Hospital Service after 1902, and finally, the United States Public Health Service in 1912." Kraut, *Silent Travelers*, 60.

2. Bolino, *The Ellis Island Source Book*, 14-15; Shapiro, *Gateway to Liberty*, 160; Pitkin, *Keepers of the Gate*, 68-69; "Ellis Island History: The Inspection Process," <www.ellisisland.com/inspection.html>.

3. Bolino, *The Ellis Island Source Book*, 14-15; Pitkin, *Keepers of the Gate*, 68-69.

4. Shapiro, *Gateway to Liberty*, 159-160; quote from Oxford, "Hope, Tears, and Remembrance," 42.

5. Chermayeff, *Ellis Island: An Illustrated History of the Immigrant Experience*, 114.

6. Shapiro, *Gateway to Liberty*, 159-160; Kraut, *Silent Travelers*, 61.

7. Bolino, *The Ellis Island Source Book*, 3; Shapiro, *Gateway to Liberty*, 160.

8. Shapiro, *Gateway to Liberty*, 165, 213; Bolino, *The Ellis Island Source Book*, 17; Oxford, "Hope, Tears, and Remembrance," 68-70; "federal officials" quote from Kraut, *Silent Travelers*, 62, number with defects from 66, see also 273; "Ellis Island History: The Inspection Process," <www.ellisisland.com/inspection.html>.

9. Letter from Josephine Massi Alford to the author, 11 May 2004, Medical Records/Health Data Supervisor, National Hansen's Disease Program, Department of Health and Human Services, 1770 Physicians Park Drive, Baton Rouge, Louisiana 70816.

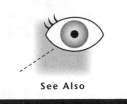

See Also

Complete citations can be found in the Bibliography, pages 153–158.

CHAPTER 9

Finding Information on Your Ancestor's Ship

F or many of us, it's not enough to see our ancestor's name on a passenger arrival list. We want to know details about the ship Great-grandma lived on for nearly two weeks while traveling to this country. Several ways are available to learn about passenger ships.

Remember Ester Ahlquist from chapter four who came over on the *Hellig Olav* in 1912? Let's look for more information on her ship. After finding Ester on the Ellis Island database, we can click on "Ship" to see a photograph of the *Hellig Olav* (or if none is available, an illustration of a typical ship of that time period is displayed), as well as details about the ship. If you'd like a print of the ship, you can order it from the EIDB site. **(If you plan to use the photograph in a published family history or on your Web site, however, you will need to obtain permission and might have to pay a fee.)**

As of this writing, you could not search on the Ellis Island database by

Reminder

Figure 9-1
Image of the *Hellig Olav* from the Ellis Island Database.

ship name only; you have to enter a passenger's name to get to the ship's list in order to view the image of the vessel. You can, however, search for a ship using Morse's "Ship Lists: Searching for Ships in the Ellis Island Microfilms in One Step" <www.stevemorse.org/ellis/boat.html>. From the main page, click on "Ship Pictures." From there, click on "Ellis Island" and type in the name of the ship. It will give you the image, but not any details about the ship. If you're uncertain how to spell the ship's name, click on "Morton Allan Directory." This will give you more search options for spellings.

Another source of information is Arnold Kludas's *Great Passenger Ships of the World*, 5 vols. (Cambridge: Stephens, 1975–1977). Volume 1: 1858–1912 has a photograph and the following information on the *Hellig Olav*:

Builders: Stephen, Glasgow

Yard no: 399

10,085 GRT; 158.5 × 17.8 m / 520 × 58.2 ft; III exp eng, Stephen; Twin screw;

8,500 IHP; 15, max 16 kn; Passengers: 130 1st class, 140 2d class, 900 steerage.

1902 Dec 16: Launched

1903 Mar 17: Delivered

　　　Mar 26: Maiden voyage Copenhagen-New York

1931 Laid up

1933 Dec: Sold for breaking-up

1934 Broken up by Hughes, Bolckow & Co., Blyth

Notice that this source gives more information than what you'd find on the EIDB. Eugene W. Smith's *Passenger Ships of the World* (Boston: George H. Dean Co., 1978) gives similar information, plus a few more details:

Hellig Olav (1902) Scandinavian-American Line.

Built by Alexander Stephen & Sons, Ltd., Glasgow, Scotland. Tonnage: 9,939. Dimensions: 500′ × 58′ (515′ o.l.). Twin-screw, 16 knots. Triple expansion engines. Two masts and one funnel. Passengers: 130 first, 140 second, 900 third. Service: Copenhagen-Oslo-New York. Final Atlantic crossing in 1931. Scrapped in 1934. Sister ships: *Oscar II* and *United States*.

You'll want to check all the sources you can, as the details may vary.

SHIPS' PHOTOGRAPHS

You'll find several other Web sites for tracking down photographs of your immigrant ancestors' ships. The National Maritime Museum <www.nmm.ac.uk> (go to "Collections & research," then scroll down to "Historic photographs catalogue") and the Mariners' Museum <www.mariner.org> (click on "Image Collection") provide assistance in obtaining photographs and sketches of ships to include when publishing a family history. Other maritime museums offering assistance are

- Mystic Seaport <www.mysticseaport.org>
- Peabody Museum of Salem <www.infonavigate.com/boston/l65.shtml>
- Steamship Historical Society of America <www.sshsa.net/index.html>

Although they don't do research, the ocean liner memorabilia Web site at <www.oceanliner.com/index.htm> sells brochures listing steamships' schedules and fares. You can also try contacting the steamship line directly, if it is still in operation. For other links, go to Maritime Museums on the Web <http://my.execpc.com/~reva/html3e2.htm>.

THE NEW YORK TIMES DATABASE

Internet Source

Another online tool for genealogists is the ProQuest Historical Newspapers database of *The New York Times*. The search engine gives you immediate access to not only the headlines and articles from 1851 to 2001, but it searches on every word of the article's text, including ads. By typing in the name of the ship your ancestor arrived on, you can find shipping news and any articles with information about that ship.

You can search *The New York Times* archives for free on the *Times* Web site <www.nytimes.com>. From the home page, either scroll down the page and click on "archive" under the services heading, or use the pull down menu to find "NYT 1851–1995" and click on the arrow. From there you'll be able to do a search similar to the one described on pages 112, 113, but you'll get only an abstract of the article. If you want to see the article, you have several choices:

1. You can see if a local public or university library has *The New York Times* on microfilm and view it for free there, or check to see if they subscribe to ProQuest Historical Newspapers database.

2. You can purchase the article from the *Times* Web site. Click on "pricing" in the menu to the right on the search page. As of this writing, a single article cost $2.95. You'll be able to view the article for ninety days in a PDF format.

3. You can become a member of either the New York Genealogical and Biographical Society <www.newyorkfamilyhistory.org> or the Godfrey Memorial Library <www.godfrey.org>, both of which subscribe to the *Times* database prepared by ProQuest. After you become a member of one of these organizations, you can view the articles in PDF files from your home computer.

SHIPPING AND MAILS

Miniature Almanac for To-day.

Sun rises..7:22|Sun sets..4:30|Moon rises...6:34

TIDES TO-DAY.

	High Water.		Low Water.	
	A.M.	P.M.	A.M.	P.M.
Sandy Hook.........	8:20	..	2:09	2:47
Governors Island....	8:44	9:15	2:35	3:16
Hell Gate...........	10:37	11:08	4:07	4:48

Arrived—Tuesday, Dec. 26.

SS Alleghany, Carthagena, Dec. 13.
SS Mesaba, London. Dec. 14.
SS El Mar, Galveston, Dec. 19.
SS Oskar II., Copenhagen. Dec. 13.
SS Allianca, Colon, Dec. 19.
SS Maracaibo, Curacao, Dec. 18.
SS Sorland, Demerara, Dec. 12.
SS Framfield, Matanzas, Dec. 13.
SS Zeeland, Antwerp, Dec. 16.
SS El Dorado, New Orleans, Dec. 20.
SS Noordam, Rotterdam, Dec. 18.
SS Firby, Algiers, Dec. 4.
SS San Jacinto, Galveston, Dec. 20.
SS Canada. Liverpool, Dec. 15.
SS Monterey, Havana, Dec. 23.

Outgoing Steamships.

SAIL TO-DAY.

	Mails Close.	Vessels Sail.
Oceanic, Liverpool......	3:00 A.M.	6:30 A.M.
Eastern Prince, Brazil..	9:00 A.M.	12:00 M.
Dagfin, Guatemala.....	10:00 A.M.	1:00 P.M.
Maranhense, Trinidad..	10:00 A.M.	1:00 P.M.
Cubana, Cuba.........	12:00 M.	3:00 P.M.
Algonquin, Charleston..	———	3:00 P.M.
Proteus, New Orleans..	———	12:00 M.
Lampasas, Galveston...	———	3:00 P.M.
Jamilton, Norfolk......	———	8:00 P.M.

SAIL TO-MORROW.

La Lorraine, Havre....	7:00 A.M.	10:00 A.M.
Bremen, Bremen........	———	10:00 A.M.
Venetia, Kingston......	11:30 A.M.	2:00 P.M.
Fontabelle, St. Thomas.	12:00 M.	3:00 P.M.
Seguranca, Havana.....	9:00 A.M.	12:00 M.
Jefferson, Norfolk......	———	3:00 P.M.

SAIL FRIDAY.

Sylvia, Newfoundland..	8:30 A.M.	11:00 A.M.
Santiago, Nassau.......	12:00 M.	3:00 P.M.
Tjomo, Campeachy.....	12:00 M.	3:00 P.M.
Jefferson, Norfolk......	———	3:00 P.M.
Sabine, Mobile.........	———	3:00 P.M.
Alamo, Brunswick......	———	3:00 P.M.

*Supplementary mails are open on the piers of the American, English, French, and German transatlantic lines until within ten minutes of the hour of sailing.

Incoming Steamships.

DUE TO-DAY.

Cherokee...............	Turk's Island..Dec.	8
Hostilius..............	Para ....Dec.	9
Sikh..................	Algiers ......Dec.	16
Giulia................	Palermo ......Dec.	6
Carpathia.............	Gibraltar .....Dec.	16
Manoa................	Demerara .....Dec.	16
Etona................	St. Lucia.....Dec.	19
Rhein................	Bremen ......Dec.	16
Maraval..............	Trinidad ......Dec.	20
El Norte..............	Galveston .....Dec.	21

DUE TO-MORROW.

Celtic................	Liverpool ......Dec.	20
Graf Waldersee.........	Hamburg ....Dec.	16
Madonna..............	Gibraltar ......Dec.	19
Prins Maurits..........	Haiti ....Dec.	22
Excelsior.............	New Orleans...Dec.	22

Reported by Wireless.

SS Celtic, incoming, was in wireless communication with the Marconi station at Cape Race at 7 P. M. yesterday, when 140 miles southeast of that point; due at her pier about 2 P. M. Friday.

SS Finland, outward bound, was in wireless communication with the Marconi station at Cape Race at 11 A. M. yesterday, when 155 miles southwest from that point.

SS Minnetonka, outward bound, was in wireless communication with the Marconi station at Cape Race at 4 P. M. yesterday, when 170 miles southeast of that point.

Figure 9-2
Shipping and mail arrival. *The New York Times*, 27 December 1905, page 14.

Figure 9-3
The New York Times, 28 October 1905, page 5.

Once you are in the ProQuest Historical Newspapers' *New York Times* database, you can do a basic search or an advanced search. Use, for example, the advanced search, and in the first field, type in the name of the ship. In the second field, type in "Ellis Island." In the date field, enter the date the ship arrived. Any articles containing the ship's name and "Ellis Island" will be listed in chronological order. For a broader search, go to the basic search page and just enter the name of the ship with dates to get every article, including arrivals, for that ship.

Using *The New York Times* Database

The Pascalis family from Greece traveled on the *Nord America*, arriving in New York on 27 October 1905. When I checked *The New York Times* database for this ship and date, I found some surprising information. The headline was "Smallpox on a Ship Passed at Quarantine. Case Discovered at Ellis Island After 2,000 Had Been Exposed." The article reported that a Greek woman among the 1,228 steerage passengers was found to have the disease. "The woman was among the last batch of steerage passengers from the *Nord America* to be examined. . . ." Although the article didn't identify the woman by name, only one Greek female passenger was aboard the *Nord America*: Cristina Pascalis. A closer look at the microfilmed list showed a faint notation in the far right margin for her listing and the passengers around her. Because it was so faint, I turned to the enhanced image on the Ellis Island database, where the notation became quite clear: "Recd from quar Nov. 11."

Outbreaks of disease on immigrant ships was a frequent topic in the *New York Times*. While articles won't typically list names of passengers, if you have the passenger list, you might be able to figure out those passengers who were affected. One of them may have been yours. So be sure to check in *The New York Times* database for all ships your ancestors arrived on.

CHAPTER 10

Leaving an Ellis Island Legacy

Y ou've learned an awful lot about your ancestor's journey to America, found the passenger list, have pictures and information about the ship, and know what it was like for him to process through Ellis Island. It's a wonderful story, and now it's time for you to tell it. **Here are some ways to record your ancestor's immigration experience:**

- Write your ancestor's story as an article, essay, or part of a family history book.
- Make a paper scrapbook.
- Make a virtual scrapbook.
- Have your immigrant ancestor's name engraved on the Ellis Island Wall of Honor.

Idea Generator

WRITING YOUR ANCESTOR'S STORY

If you like to write and want to preserve your ancestor's experience on paper, here are some topics you can research and write about:

- **Homeland.** Describe the lifestyle there, the geography, the types of houses, the climate, different occupations, predominant religion, and so forth.
- **Motivation to Leave.** What pushed your ancestors to leave? Did the husband come first and bring his wife and family later? Was he a bird of passage? Did the whole family come together? Was there someone already in America who likely enticed them to emigrate?
- **Shipboard Experience.** What kind of vessel did they travel on? Sailing or steam? How long did the voyage take? What occupied their time during the voyage? How many people could the ship hold? How many actually traveled with your ancestors?
- **Arrival and Processing.** Where did your ancestors arrive? Did they come

For More Info

For more on writing family histories, see Sharon De-Bartolo Carmack's *You Can Write Your Family History* (Cincinnati: Betterway Books, 2003).

before or after federal immigrant processing was initiated? If after, what was it like to process through Castle Garden or Ellis Island?

- **Settlement and Internal Migration.** Where did your immigrant ancestors initially settle and why? Where and with whom did they live when they got here? Did they live in an ethnic enclave or cluster around others from their homeland? How long did they stay in a given area? Where did they go after this place? How did they get there?
- **New Environment.** Describe the lifestyle in their new environment in America, the geography, the types of houses, the climate, and so forth. How similar or dissimilar was it to their homeland? What kind of work did they do? Was this the same type of work they did in the homeland?
- **Assimilation.** How were they treated once they got here? Were they eager to become naturalized? Did they join fraternal benefit societies? What church did they attend? What newspapers did they read? Did they anglicize or change their names? Did they send their children to school? Did the immigrant's daughters or sons marry outside the ethnic group?

The answers to practically all these questions will come from your genealogical research, from oral history interviews, from home sources, and from social histories, where you can learn what the typical experience was like for other members of the same ethnic group who lived during the same time period as your ancestors and who settled in the same areas. For example, I don't know the exact experience of my great-grandparents who came from Italy and were processed through Ellis Island in the early 1900s, but I can still write about it in factual detail. From reading social histories on the immigrant experience at Ellis Island (such as in chapter seven), I can portray what it was probably like for my own ancestors and still keep it an authentic account.

Here I have paraphrased the general, typical Ellis Island experience, as written about in Thomas M. Pitkin's *Keepers of the Gate: A History of Ellis Island* (pp. 68-69):

> At the first station in the huge Registry Hall, a surgeon checked each arrival's health inspection card from aboard ship. After stamping it, he handed it back to the immigrant and watched. The unsuspecting person would look to see what the inspector had stamped on the card and would inadvertently reveal any eye problems.

You could summarize and cite material as I've just done, or you can weave your ancestor's story into it:

> At the first station in the huge Registry Hall, a surgeon checked each arrival's health inspection card from aboard ship, and he *no doubt* checked Salvatore Ebetino's, too. After stamping it, the surgeon *would have handed* it back to Salvatore and watched. The unsuspecting immigrant *probably*

\di'fin\ *vb*

Definitions

Social histories examine the everyday lives of ordinary people.

looked to see what the inspector had stamped on the card, and Salvatore *would have* inadvertently revealed any eye problems.

Note the language in italics that clearly indicates that I'm speculating on Salvatore's experience. Unless I have documented proof that this is what actually happened to Salvatore, I can't word the paragraph as if it were fact.

For it to be a factual narrative, not only do you want to make it clear when you speculate about experiences that *probably* happened to your ancestors, but you also want to include source citations, or as we genealogists say, documentation. **The rules are simple: For every fact, cite a source where that fact came from.** If you say that Salvatore Ebetino came on the *Italia* in 1906, that's a fact that requires documentation. Where did that information come from? The other rule is to cite as much information about the source as necessary for you or another researcher to find that source again. The citation for the Ebetino passenger arrival list is:

Supplies

> Ebetino, Salvatore. *Italia*, departing Naples 25 April 1906, arriving New York 10 May 1906, group 7, list 137, line 6, NARA Microfilm Publication T715, roll 706, vol. 1564.

Put your documentation in footnotes or endnotes grouped at the end of the story.

Figure 10-1
Photo courtesy of the Ellis Island Immigration Museum.

CREATING AN IMMIGRANT SCRAPBOOK

Several books and magazines on the market can teach you how to make scrapbooks and recommend where to purchase scrapbooking items. If you want to make a scrapbook to honor your immigrant ancestor, here are some items to consider including:

- photograph of the ancestor
- photograph of the ship
- the passenger arrival list
- a photograph of Ellis Island
- short descriptions about the journey and the Ellis Island experience
- memorabilia from the immigrant experience, such as the passenger ticket and inspection cards
- naturalization papers

For More Info

For more on making heritage scrapbooks, see Maureen A. Taylor's *Scrapbooking Your Family History* (Cincinnati: Betterway Books, 2003).

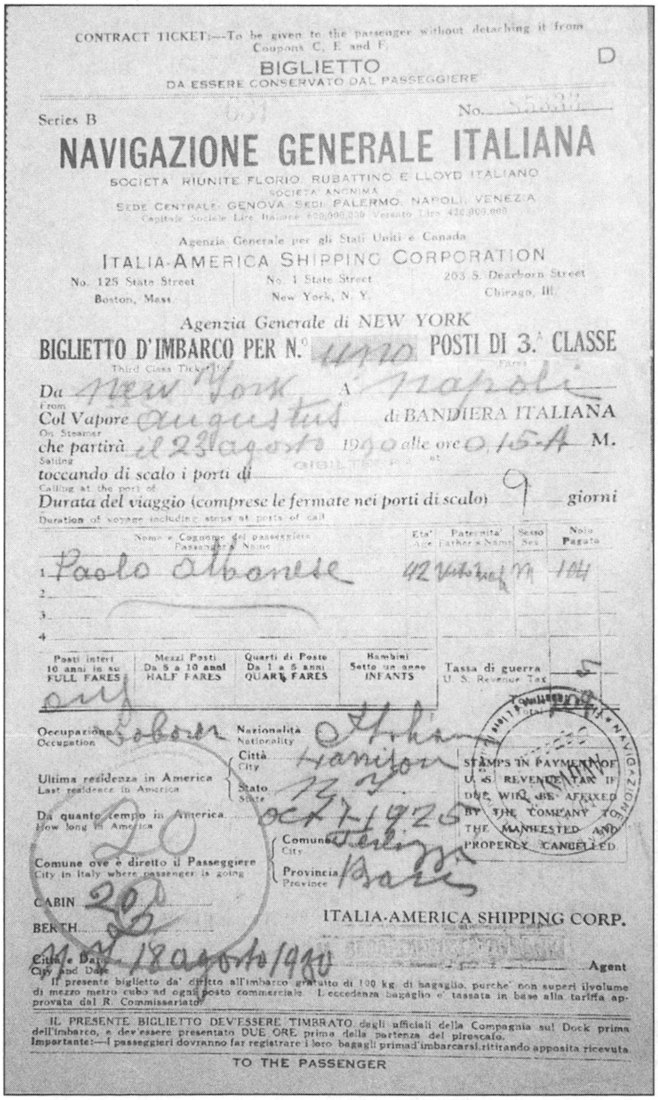

CONTRACT TICKET:—To be given to the passenger without detaching it from Coupons C, E and F.
D
BIGLIETTO
DA ESSERE CONSERVATO DAL PASSEGGIERE

Series B — No.

NAVIGAZIONE GENERALE ITALIANA
SOCIETA' RIUNITE FLORIO RUBATTINO E LLOYD ITALIANO
SOCIETA' ANONIMA
SEDE CENTRALE: GENOVA SEDI: PALERMO, NAPOLI, VENEZIA

Agenzia Generale per gli Stati Uniti e Canada
ITALIA-AMERICA SHIPPING CORPORATION
No. 125 State Street, Boston, Mass. — No. 1 State Street, New York, N. Y. — 203 S. Dearborn Street, Chicago, Ill.

Agenzia Generale di NEW YORK
BIGLIETTO D'IMBARCO PER N.° 11110 POSTI DI 3.^ CLASSE
Third Class Ticket for — Fares
Da (From) New York A (to) Napoli
Col Vapore (On Steamer) Augustus di BANDIERA ITALIANA
che partirà (Sailing) il 23 agosto 1930 alle ore (at) 0.15 A. M.
toccando di scalo i porti di (Calling at the port of) GIBILTERRA
Durata del viaggio (comprese le fermate nei porti di scalo) (Duration of voyage including stops at ports of call) 9 giorni

	Nome e Cognome del passeggiere / Passenger's Name	Eta' / Age	Paternita' / Father's Name	Sesso / Sex	Nolo Pagato
1	Paolo Albanese	42		M	104
2					
3					
4					

Posti interi 10 anni in su FULL FARES	Mezzi Posti Da 5 a 10 anni HALF FARES	Quarti di Posto Da 1 a 5 anni QUART. FARES	Bambini Sotto un anno INFANTS	Tassa di guerra U. S. Revenue Tax
one				5

Total

Occupazione (Occupation) Laborer
Nazionalità (Nationality) Italian
Ultima residenza in America (Last residence in America): Città (City) Harrison; Stato (State) N.Y.
Da quanto tempo in America (How long in America) Oct 1-1925
Comune ove è diretto il Passeggiere (City in Italy where passenger is going): Comune (City); Provincia (Province) Bari

STAMPS IN PAYMENT OF U. S. REVENUE TAX IF DUE, WILL BE AFFIXED BY THE COMPANY TO THE MANIFESTED AND PROPERLY CANCELLED.

CABIN 20
BERTH

ITALIA-AMERICA SHIPPING CORP.
Agent

Città e Data (City and Date) N.Y. 18 agosto 1930

Il presente biglietto da' diritto all'imbarco gratuito di 100 kg. di bagaglio, purche' non superi il volume di mezzo metro cubo ad ogni posto commerciale. L'eccedenza bagaglio e' tassata in base alla tariffa approvata dal R. Commissariato.

IL PRESENTE BIGLIETTO DEV'ESSERE TIMBRATO dagli ufficiali della Compagnia sul Dock prima dell'imbarco, e dev'essere presentato DUE ORE prima della partenza del piroscafo.
Importante:—I passeggieri dovranno far registrare i loro bagagli prima d'imbarcarsi, ritirando apposita ricevuta.

TO THE PASSENGER

Figure 10-2
Steamship ticket purchased by Paolo Albanese for third class fare on the *Augustus*, departing from New York on 28 August 1930 to Naples, Italy. Family momentos like this are perfect for scrapbooks. But use a copy in the scrapbook. Preserve the original in an archival-quality sheet protector.

Remember, if you have original documents in your possession, make photo-copies to put in the scrapbook and preserve the originals.

VIRTUAL SCRAPBOOKS

You can create a virtual scrapbook on the Ellis Island Web site, but you must be a Foundation member to do so. Once you become a member, you'll receive instructions that will walk you through creating an online scrapbook of photographs and text.

You can search the site without becoming a Foundation member to see if someone has already created a scrapbook on your family. From the Ellis Island home page, click on "Family Scrapbooks," then on "Search Scrapbooks." You'll be able to search by title, keyword, or member names. When typing in the surname Russo, for example, two matches were found: one for the Russo/Lo Russo Family History and one for the Savino Family History. Both scrapbooks contained sixty-one pages of photographs and family history.

Figure 10-3
Russo/Lo Russo Family History scrapbook on Ellis Island Web site.

AMERICAN IMMIGRANT WALL OF HONOR

The American Immigrant Wall of Honor, a national monument located on Ellis Island, is a way to honor those who came to this country. It's not limited to ancestors who came through Ellis Island; any immigrant's name is eligible. For a fee ($100 taxable donation as of this writing), you can add your ancestor's name to the wall online by going to the American Immigrant Wall of Honor Web site <www.wallofhonor.com>. From this site, you can also search to see if someone has already placed your ancestor's name on the wall.

Figure 10-4
Immigrant Wall of Honor on Ellis Island.

Oral History

ELLIS ISLAND'S ORAL HISTORY PROJECT

To hear about the voyage and experience of processing through Ellis Island in the immigrants' own words, **visit the Ellis Island Museum to access hundreds of taped oral history interviews with immigrants and staff.**

Eight microfilm reels contain hundreds of original oral history transcripts, "Voices from Ellis Island: An Oral History of American Immigration." These are available through the Family History Library in Salt Lake City, Utah, or through loan at a Family History Center. On the FamilySearch.org site, click on the library catalog. From there, do a subject search on "Ellis Island Immigration Station." In the results, click on "Ellis Island Immigration Station (New York, New York)." Then click on "Voices from Ellis Island. . . ." You'll view a description of the collection, but if you go to "View Film Notes," you'll get even more details, including the names of those interviewed and their origins.

Whether you write your immigrant ancestors' stories, make a scrapbook, or have their names engraved on the Wall of Honor, you're leaving a legacy. You, the family historian, have the responsibility not only to learn about your ancestors through research but to pass that information along to future generations. On a chart, Salvatore and Angelina Ebetino are just names. In a narrative or scrapbook, they become people. You've gone through all the time, expense, and trouble to get to know your ancestors, to appreciate what it took for them to leave behind loved ones and their country, to settle in a strange land. What a terrible waste and injustice it would be to leave them as just names on a chart. Share the stories of your immigrant ancestors. They deserve to be remembered. They are, after all, part of American history.

The Creation and Destruction of Ellis Island Immigration Manifests, Part 1

By Marian L. Smith

Reprinted with permission of the author. Both parts originally published in *Prologue* 28 (Fall and Winter 1996): 240-45, 314-18, respectively.

Notes

Endnotes begin on page 123.

F ederal immigration manifests, also known as passenger arrival lists, are among the most popular records at the National Archives and Records Administration (NARA). Researchers using microfilm copies of Immigration and Naturalization Service (INS) passenger arrival records are not always satisfied with the film's quality or legibility and often ask the NARA or INS for access to the original paper manifest. Such frequent requests prompted an investigation into INS's decision to destroy its original records. The result is new insight into the immigration agency's use of passenger lists and the legacy of the Records Act of 1943. This article recounts Ellis Island manifests' life in paper form and their preservation on microfilm. Part 2, in the Winter 1996 issue of *Prologue* [on page 126 of this book], will explain the fate of the original lists.

The federal government began collecting immigration records in 1820 under a law designed to regulate shipping lines carrying immigrants to the United States. The Steerage Act of 1819 required the captain or master of any ship or vessel arriving in the United States to deliver a passenger manifest to a federal official. In those years, the Treasury Department oversaw such matters, and the United States Customs Collector at each port collected passenger manifests as well as cargo manifests. Known as "customs manifests," these lists were to provide each passenger's name, age, sex, occupation, and nationality. The Immigration Act of March 3, 1891, established the Office of Immigration and the Immigration Service within the Treasury Department. After that date, a U.S. Immigration official gathered all passenger manifests, now known as "immigration manifests" after the agency that collected them.[1]

The 1891 law added two items to the manifest: the last residence of the alien and his or her final destination in the United States. During the early twentieth century, Congress extended the list of required manifest information three times. The Immigration Act of March 3, 1903, stipulated eleven more items; the act of February 20, 1907, one more; and the act of February 5, 1917, six more. This data, which included information about an immigrant's previous home, family, and relations in the United States, has obvious value for family history research.

While various immigration laws increased the information collected on manifests, successive legislation also imposed specifications on the format and completion of manifest forms. The Immigration Act of 1893 required listing immigrants in "convenient groups" of no more than thirty names per page. Immigration Service officers interpreted convenient groups to be members of the same family or those coming from the same town or village. This law also mandated the practice, for inspection purposes, of issuing passengers numbered tickets that corresponded to the page and line number where their name appeared on the manifest.[2]

Transportation companies had to provide the manifest forms, and regulations under the Immigration Act of 1917 mandated the forms' size, color, and quality of paper. All immigration manifests were to be typed or printed in English. Typed manifests were to use 36″ × 18½″ sheets designated as Form 500. Different colored forms applied to each class of passengers: first class on pink manifests (Form 500), second class on yellow (Form 500A), and steerage on white (Form 500B). Printed sheets were to be either 36″ × 18½″ or 18″ × 18½″. The smaller sheets were Form 630 (pink), 630A (yellow), and 630B (white).[3]

The U.S. Bureau of Immigration also furnished transportation companies with blank books to prepare alphabetical indexes and facilitate reference to the manifests. It is unclear when the INS first provided such index books to the companies, how long they did so, or if it intended for the company to submit the index with the manifest. A footnote to the regulations of 1921 states simply that "[t]he practice . . . shall be continued." Years later, the Immigration Service microfilmed the alphabetical index books as well as the manifests.[4]

Ship manifests served as the Immigration Service's sole official arrival record for documentation of each admissible immigrant. As such, the manifests were the foundation of inspection procedure and provided the raw data for official immigration statistics. The INS adopted a punch-card system to collect statistics during the earliest years of the twentieth century (probably as early as 1907). Using "punch machines," immigration clerks in the field converted manifest data to coded holes in cards and forwarded them to the central office for tabulation.[5]

After the clerks used the manifests for inspection and statistical purposes, they sent them to the station or port's record unit for storage and future reference. Pre–World War II laws and rules regulating the Immigration Service contained no specifics about how those documents were to be filed. The Immigration Service filed manifests at each port just as the Customs Service had since 1819—by date of arrival, then by name of vessel.

Field offices then had their manifests bound into books of about 150 sheets, usually contracting with a local printer or bookbinder to do so. Manifest book spines were typically glued, but many were subsequently nailed, riveted, or stitched to hold the covers and pages together.[6] Clerks numbered the books as volumes, then placed them in "bins" or some other sort of shelving. Beginning on December 1, 1924, records personnel at Ellis Island bound all the New York manifests in loose-leaf binders, each binder holding an average of 150 sheets arranged by date of arrival. The binders, too, continued to be consecutively numbered as volumes. One officer of the Immigration Service reported that Ellis Island manifests covering the period from December 1924 to December 1942 filled 6,121 binders. A 1943 document reported the entire collection of manifest volumes stored at Ellis Island numbered 14,100.[7]

Ellis Island officials, like those at other immigration ports of entry, did not send their manifests to the central office in Washington, D.C., because the records were needed for daily use in arrival verification work. Officers might request proof of an immigrant's legal entry (arrival) for a variety of reasons. For example, all applications for Reentry Permits, Certificates of Arrival, or other benefits required checking an application against the original arrival record. As a consequence of the manifest filing system, all requests for verification of arrival had to include the port, date of arrival, and name of vessel, as well as an alien's full name and other identifying information. Search requests of direct arrivals to known ports of entry required only the identifying information, date of arrival, and name of vessel.[8]

Upon receipt of a request for verification of an alien's arrival, clerks went first to the index book for the specified vessel and date. There the clerk learned the volume, page, and line that contained information about the alien named in the request. The clerk then went to the reference room, found the volume, and placed it on a nearby table. After locating the alien's name on the page, he transcribed the information from the manifest onto a slip of paper. The clerk returned to the office and typed the handwritten information onto the proper or desired form.[9]

By the mid-1930s, when the earliest volumes were forty years old, this system of arrival verification began to pose problems for the Immigration Service. The documents' age and constant use caused deterioration of the paper and ink. As one Ellis Island official explained, "[e]ach evening, after a day's reference work, it was not unusual to observe fragments of pages lying on the floor. Most of these fragments were too small to identify and had to be thrown away. Records of extreme value to the Service as working implements were thus being lost . . . and many pages were rapidly reaching a stage where further rebinding was impossible."[10]

A high possibility of error in service operations resulted from the problems of disintegration, fading ink, and the necessity of researching and typing at different locations. That procedure also held few safeguards against the problem of fraud, especially on Ellis Island. Personal contact between Immigration Service employees and "runners" provided ample opportunity for bribes, and the verification process could be abused to create false documents.[11]

Beginning in November 1935, Works Progress Administration (WPA) workers employed in an indexing project attempted repairs to many of the Ellis Island manifests. They reconstructed and reinforced damaged sheets with "gummed" cellulose acetate and manila tape. Such measures, however, were not adequate for the preservation job ahead.

In late summer 1942, the INS consulted with the National Archives regarding possible methods of rehabilitating or preserving immigration arrival records. The service first considered laminating the sheets but decided this would be impractical because it would double the size and weight of the volumes. Records officers also debated and rejected proposals to photograph the records or to transcribe them manually. By the following spring, INS officers concluded that "[m]icrofilming seemed the nearest approach to the solution of all of our problems."[12]

Many sound arguments justified microfilming of the ship manifests. That process would preserve the records—the service's original motive—and reduce the likelihood of error or fraud. Another advantage of microfilm became apparent in 1942, soon after the United States entered into World War II. Until that time, it had always "been the policy of the Service to employ men" as verification clerks because of the bulk and weight (approximately twenty pounds each) of manifest volumes. Several microfilmed volumes weighed only a few ounces, a weight women could certainly lift, and constituted "another reason, in view of the present shortage of male labor, why microfilming is a necessity now."[13]

An additional reason for microfilming the manifests became clear in 1943 when the INS moved its New York administrative functions from Ellis Island to 70 Columbus Avenue in Manhattan. During World War II the service, like every federal agency and department, experienced a shortage of office space. Although the INS had taken over the entire building at 70 Columbus Avenue (formerly occupied by the WPA), INS officers in Washington were concerned that the manifest records occupied twenty-five thousand square feet of floor space in the new facility.[14]

The space problem plagued nearly every federal agency, as did the mounting problem of records storage. Congress responded with the Records Act of July 7, 1943, which provided government agencies with a framework for records management. Official records could be transformed into other, more permanent forms (such as microfilm) or could be retired and stored in federal records centers, where space was less expensive. Equally important, the act also included procedures for destruction of useless or duplicate records. The Records Act certainly offered relief to the INS, which had recently created or obtained many millions of new records as a result of various war-related programs.[15]

By 1943 New York manifests constituted 60 percent of all INS arrival records. Under the Records Act, INS officers decided to use the New York arrival records as a pilot program. If microfilm copies of manifests proved satisfactory for verification work, the originals would be destroyed, and the service would reduce storage expenses. Accordingly, INS contracted a microfilming firm to duplicate all the New York manifests. As part of the agreement, the contractors trained two INS employees during the project to microfilm records at other ports. Filming began in July 1943, took more than a year to complete, and cost approximately $200,000. They made two copies of the records (one for the INS and one for the National Archives) to prevent any future loss by fire. Microfilmed manifests occupied only five hundred square feet of space in the 70 Columbus Avenue building (2 percent of the original volume).[16]

With the manifests preserved on microfilm for verification work, INS officials in Washington prepared to destroy the originals under provisions of the Records Act.

Endnotes

1. Act of March 2, 1819 (Steerage Act), §4; All surviving customs manifests were turned over to the National Archives, where they were microfilmed (microfilm copies are also available at other private institutions). In or around 1974, the Archives transferred the original (paper) customs manifests to the Temple University-Balch Institute Center for Immigration Research. Because the new Immigration Service did not have inspectors at all U.S. ports, many customs inspectors were designated to do immigration inspections as well. While ship captains continued to submit manifests to customs officials at those ports, the records are considered immigration manifests.

2. Immigration Act of March 3, 1891, §8; Act of March 3, 1893, §1-2; Immigration Act of 1917, §13, and 42, rule 2, subdivision 2, *Immigration Laws [and] Rules of May 1, 1917*, 6th ed., September 1921 (1921), pp. 14-15.

3. Rule 2, subdivision 1, *Immigration Laws [and] Rules of May 1, 1917*, 7th ed., August 1922 (1922), p. 48; rule 2(C)(2), *Immigration Laws and Rules of February 1, 1924* (1924), p. 111.

4. For the alphabetical indexes, see *Book Indexes to New York Passenger Lists, 1906–1942* (National Archives Microfilm Publication T612, 807 rolls), Records of the Immigration and Naturalization Service, Record Group 85, National Archives, Washington, D.C. (hereinafter, records in the National Archives will be cited as RG__, NA); The book indexes are grouped by shipping line and then arranged chronologically by the date of arrival. The same statement appears in a 1922 edition of the same regulations but is not reprinted in subsequent editions. Rule 2, subdivision 1, fn. 2, *Immigration Laws [and] Rules of May 1, 1917*, 6th ed., September 1921 (1921) p. 42; Interviews with Ira Glazer, Apr. 3, 1992; Sharon Mahoney, INS Verification Center, Martinsburg, W.V., Apr. 7, 1992 (telephone); and Constance Potter, Genealogy Specialist, National Archives and Records Administration, Washington, D.C., Apr. 9, 1992 (telephone).

5. Tabulation equipment was also installed on Ellis Island, the largest immigration station, by 1912. "Immigration and Naturalization Statistics of the United States—Their Nature, Volume, and Method of Compilation," by J. J. Kunna and H. L. Stanforth (Statistical Division, INS), Jan. 7, 1935, *INS Lecture Series* [2d Series] Number 30, p. 6; The subject index to subject files provided what is known about installation of Hollerith machines on Ellis Island.

6 The subject index to the 56000 Series of records includes many references to contracts and expenditures for the binding of manifests at field offices. For the condition of the manifest books, see Len G. Townsend, "The Microfilming of Arrival Records in the New York District Office of the Immigration and Naturalization Service," typescript, Nov. 18, 1944, in INS File 56134/715, "NY Manifest Microfilming, 1942–1952," box 10, accession 85-58A0734, Immigration and Naturalization Service. See also "The Service Microfilms Its Ellis Island Records," [INS] *Monthly Review* 1 (August 1943): 23-24; and "The Microfilm Project in New York," *Monthly Review* 1 (May 1944): 12.

7 Memorandum, INS New York District Administrative Services Officer Ralph H. Holton to Director of Administrative Services Perry M. Oliver, May 12, 1945; memorandum ("Inspection of Ships' Manifests of the Port of New York stored at Ellis Island by the Immigration and Naturalization Service"), Adelaide E. Minogue (Acting Chief, Division of Repair and Preservation) to Director of Records, Accessioning and Preservation, Apr. 14, 1943, INS file 56134/713. The "bins" at Ellis Island were metal shelving that filled the large reference room. Townsend, "The Microfilming of Arrival Records," p. 1, INS file 56134/715.

8 Ralph H. Horner (Supervisor, Reentry and Exit Permit Unit), "Immigration and Naturalization Documents, Records, and Indexes," May 1, 1943. INS, *Course of Study for Members of the Service* (unpubl. ms., 1943 [INS History Library, Washington, D.C.]), p. 2. After July 1, 1924, visa files housed at the central office also documented an alien's arrival. During the late 1930s, the visa files were indexed under the Soundex system. The visa index has allowed name searching *for those immigrants who arrived after July 1, 1924.*

9 The customary form for this purpose was a Certificate of Admission of Alien, Form 505 (after 1942, Form I-404).

10 Townsend, "Microfilming of Arrival Records," pp. 1-2, INS file 56134/715.

11 Ibid.; "Memorandum for Mr. Savoretti," from Operations Advisor Ernest E. Salisbury to Deputy Commissioner Joseph Savoretti, Nov. 27, 1943, INS file 56134/715.

12 WPA Program of Research & Record Reorganization for the United States Immigration & Naturalization Service, Division of Community Service Programs, Planning & Control Section, Program Information Series No. 2 (1941), pp. 3, 4.

13 "The Service Microfilms Its Ellis Island Records," *Monthly Review* 1 (August 1943): 23.

14 Ibid., and INS Annual Report, 1943, p. 26.

15 Act of July 7, 1943 (PL 115, 78th Cong., 1st sess.); "Administrative History of the Immigration & Naturalization Service During World War II," Aug. 19, 1946, (unpubl. ms., INS History Library, Washington, D.C.), pp. 63-64. World War II programs included alien registration, internment of aliens of enemy nationality, and military naturalization.

16 Ibid.

Information Added to Ship Passenger Lists by Various U.S. Immigration Laws Required by Act of March 2, 1819

Name
Age
Sex
Occupation
Nationality

Added by Act of March 3, 1891

Last residence
Final destination

Added by Act of March 3, 1903

Marital status
Previous residence in U.S.
Relative/friend at destination
Literacy
Ticketed to destination
Who paid for passage
Funds in possession
Ever institutionalized for crime or insanity
Whether a polygamist or anarchist
State of health
Race

Added by Act of February 20, 1907

Relative/friend in home country

Added by Act of February 5, 1917

Personal description (height, complexion, hair and eye color, identifying
    marks)
Place of birth

The Creation and Destruction of Ellis Island Immigration Manifests, Part 2

By Marian L. Smith

During World War II, the Immigration and Naturalization Service (INS) launched a microfilm project to preserve the agency's immigrant arrival records (see Fall 1996 *Prologue*). Top INS officials then announced a plan to save space and reduce costs by destroying the original paper manifests. For the next three and a half years, managers at the INS Central Office in Washington, D.C., and at the INS District Office in New York debated the decision to destroy original records. In addition to explaining why no paper immigration manifests survive, this episode reminds us of the bureaucratic difficulties involved in implementing new national policy, the ability of resourceful field officers to resist that policy, and how unexpected, disinterested outsiders (in this case, the Atomic Energy Commission) can influence the course of events.

Notes

Endnotes begin on page 131.

Joseph Savoretti, deputy commissioner of immigration and naturalization, began the effort to dispose of original manifests in May 1944 with a memorandum to Commissioner Earl G. Harrison. Savoretti explained that, under the law, microfilm had the same force as original records, and under those circumstances, he saw no reason to retain the manifests and index books occupying "practically an entire floor" of the INS building in New York City. Savoretti recommended destruction of the old records and of all new manifests when they were microfilmed. He even attached a National Archives approval form for Commissioner Harrison to sign. Apparently in no mood to be rash, Harrison responded by asking that the whole proposal be cleared through INS Administrative Services and the National Archives.[1]

Savoretti enlisted the help of INS Director of Administrative Services Perry M. Oliver, who then asked New York District Director W. Frank Watkins for any "good reason" not to carry out the planned destruction of the passenger lists. The question clearly took Watkins by surprise. He reminded Oliver that in all previous discussions of the microfilming project, intended as a preservation project, there was no indication that the originals would be destroyed. Furthermore, the district director thought records personnel in New York needed more experience with the microfilm before they could determine if the originals were now unnecessary. As to the need for space, Watkins said there was no pressing need for the room now occupied by manifests and saw no reason to destroy them. "The original records," he concluded, "are irreplaceable and their hasty destruction would be most unfortunate, in my opinion." For the moment, Watkins's argument prevailed. Oliver decided to take no action unless a need arose for additional space at the New York District Office.[2]

The issue faded away for the summer, but in late September, officials at the Central Office met again to arrange for destruction of the New York manifests. During the meeting, Oliver asked Administrative Analyst Leonard G. Townsend to prepare answers to two serious objections "against our plan." First, Townsend noted that the Bureau of the Budget regarded space as a critical item in federal expenditures and the INS would not be able to justify retaining the space for storage of unused records. Second, he answered the argument that it was easier to detect fraud on the originals than on the microfilm. It had been at least eight years since they found any fraud in the arrival records, and he thought few more cases would ever come to light. Townsend stressed the prevention of future fraud rather than detection of past irregularities. No one could alter microfilm records, and that fact made microfilm preferable to original manifests.[3]

Meanwhile, Joseph Savoretti, who was by this time acting commissioner of immigration and naturalization, tried again to get District Director Watkins to support destruction of the manifests. Savoretti said one of the reasons for microfilming was the ability to dispose of the original manifests. He acknowledged that Watkins might have space to store the records but thought the INS would be "justifiably criticized" for retaining originals after spending public funds for their preservation on microfilm.[4]

After meeting with Perry Oliver in early October, Watkins sent another memorandum to Savoretti explaining why he still thought it wrong to destroy the original manifests. He was not yet convinced that the INS would not need the records in verification or some other sort of work. "Microfilms at the best are merely copies of original documents," Watkins concluded, and he was of "the firm opinion that the records themselves, accumulated over long years of operation, should be preserved until no question remains as to whether it is desirable to retain or to destroy them."[5]

There was perhaps another reason why Watkins did not wish to rely upon microfilm copies, though he did not mention it in his correspondence. During July 1943, when the first reels of microfilm had just come into use in New York City, clerks opened the windows to provide relief from the heat of the reader machines. By August the microfilm operation experienced problems caused by "the excessive amount of dust and cinders . . . settling on these machines from the open windows." Dirt particles found their way into the readers, leaving the film "very dirty and badly scratched from just normal use." The INS prevented further harm to the microfilm by isolating and air-conditioning the microfilm room, but the fact that the film had been damaged by unforeseen circumstances may have caused Watkins to doubt the permanency of such records.[6]

Back at the Central Office in Washington, Savoretti and Oliver continued their effort to destroy the manifests and thereby prevent any criticism for maintaining two sets of records. Oliver decided to destroy the records on January 1, 1945, because that date would be six weeks after the contractor's delivery of the last microfilms. New York records personnel would then have six weeks' experience with the entire microfilm set. Already, New York reported that for the last five months verification clerks had not had occasion to refer to original manifests. Oliver saw no reason to preserve the originals. In fact, he said he only delayed disposal until January 1 because he thought it "justifiable in view of the deep-seated feeling on the part of Mr. Watkins about the whole subject."[7]

Savoretti then offered Watkins one more chance to make the manifest decision unanimous. The acting commissioner admitted the original purpose in microfilming was not to save space but to preserve the records. The project achieved that goal. The manifests were preserved, and the microfilm now served for verification purposes. Savoretti said he and others at Central Office had discussed the issue again and again, and "none of us can perceive any justifiable excuse for maintaining the two sets of records." Rather, he expected that keeping the original manifests would bring "considerable criticism" from both the Bureau of the Budget and the Justice Department.[8]

Watkins felt betrayed. When planning the microfilm project in 1943, Central Office had assured him that no decision had been made as to destruction of the manifests and that when the question did come up, Central Office would take no "hasty action . . . nor would this office be hurried in reaching a conclusion." Now, even before the contractor delivered all the microfilm, and after only a few months' experience using the film for verification work, officials in Washington wanted him to join them in a rush to destroy official government records. Watkins was not persuaded. The district director remained firm in his objection and his warning that the INS would regret "doing away with such valuable and irresplaceable [sic] documents." Watkins pleaded for preservation of the original records:

> As I view it, no one can undertake to say at this time that some very vital need may not develop for frequent reference to these records in the future, for a number of reasons which can not be foreseen at this time. As previously stated, microfilms are merely copies of original documents and to destroy the latter beyond any possibility of recall when there has been no adequate opportunity to ascertain whether such destruction is in the public interest, would, it seems to me, be a grievous mistake.

Watkins offered a compromise solution. He determined that all the New York manifests and index books could be stored in 15,322 cubic feet of space, and he offered to store them in the basement of the INS building in Manhattan or in INS's ample space on Ellis Island.[9] It was a futile gesture, since Savoretti already admitted that the space issue was not Central Office's only motivation.

Two days later, Savoretti ordered Oliver to take the question to Acting INS General Counsel Albert E. Reitzel for confirmation of the argument Savoretti used in July 1943, when he tried to persuade Commissioner Harrison to sign off on destruction of the records. He wanted the general counsel to provide a legal opinion "as to whether or not the microfilm records are admissible evidence in lieu of the originals." If Reitzel confirmed that microfilm would meet the rules of evidence, Savoretti would proceed with his plan to destroy the originals on January 1, 1945.[10]

Reitzel understood the request. After three weeks, he delivered his opinion in a memorandum to Oliver. It was a simple discussion and explanation of Section 13 of the Records Act of July 7, 1943, that clearly stated that photographs and microphotographs of official records "shall be treated as originals" for legal purposes. Only at the end of the memorandum did Reitzel supply the answer Savoretti really wanted, when he noted "that if the original records are not destroyed and there is no showing made in the court that they are destroyed, there may be instances where the courts would only consider the original records as admissible in evidence."[11]

If maintaining original records meant the INS still had to provide original documents to the courts, the service could not afford to keep the originals. From the beginning, the New York manifest microfilming was a pilot project under the Records Act. The INS hoped to microfilm and destroy a multitude of records kept at numerous offices throughout the country. If Central Office allowed District Director Watkins to prevent destruction of manifests in New York, then other officials might prevent the destruction of many other records nationwide. To ensure success of the entire records management program, the Immigration and Naturalization Service had no choice but to order destruction of the manifests.

While Watkins was no doubt aware of Central Office's larger goals, he had not given up his fight. When Deputy Commissioner Thomas B. Shoemaker visited the New York District on February 21, 1945, Watkins prevailed upon him to intercede on the manifests' behalf. Shoemaker immediately ordered Oliver to delay "destruction of those records until I have an opportunity to discuss the matter further with the Commissioner." Shoemaker apparently made a convincing case when he finally met with Commissioner Ugo Carusi, because a mid-March memorandum to the file reported that Carusi decided "the matter should be left 'status quo.'"[12]

Administrative officers in Washington had to wait for another opportunity to destroy the New York manifests, but they did not have to wait long. By early May, Oliver learned that New York had submitted a requisition for two hundred new manifest binders. He returned the requisition and suggested that New York empty two hundred binders containing manifests already microfilmed. The removed pages could be tied up with string and stored, the binders reused, and the INS spared the expense of purchasing new binders.

After New York's Administrative Services officer resisted this idea, Central Office prepared an accounting of just how much money the INS could save if salvageable binders from New York (five thousand of them) could be used to supply all future requisitions for binders from INS offices nationwide.[13]

The numbers projected an ultimate savings of $12,500, a fact that finally moved Commissioner Carusi. In a memorandum of May 23, he explained that the New York manifests had been spared because they put no burden on the service. "If, however, their retention is to prevent our use of the binders which are needed elsewhere and which must be replaced by purchase, the jig is up, and the next two paragraphs [disposal procedures] come into merciless operation." The commissioner directed Watkins to macerate the manifests and report to Central Office as to how many binders became available for INS use. He then told an INS management officer that if he saw "many more memo's on N.Y. manifests, I shall make careful arrangements to become psycopathic [sic]."[14]

Commissioner Carusi was mistaken if he expected Watkins to destroy the manifests. Just days after Carusi's memorandum, New York Office records managers moved to preserve the original records by recommending their permanent retention:

> These are the original records of arriving passengers which show in red and blue ink the notations of the inspectors who examined the passengers, these notations having specified significance. In microfilming the records, the notations appear in black only. There are occasions when it is advisable to refer to the original record to correctly interpret entries of the examining inspector. Other reasons may develop for requiring the original records. We know now that the courts frequently call for the original records, rather than the microfilmed records. The retention of these records does not create a space problem. We strongly recommend the retention of these records for an indefinite period.[15]

In response to the commissioner's memorandum, the New York Administrative Services officer notified Central Office of his "interpretation that this district may retain manifests already microfilmed, provided the binders . . . are made available for reuse." He emptied two hundred binders and bound the old manifest pages with wrapping paper and string. Commissioner Carusi approved this solution as long as New York would supply any INS office in need of additional binders.[16]

Despite every effort by INS administrative officers, the New York manifests remained indestructible. At least it seemed that way for the next two years, until December 1947, when the commissioner received a memorandum from the New York District's new administrative officer, Trent Doser. The Atomic Energy Commission was moving into the New York District office building and required both the fifth and sixth floors. To free up this space, Doser thought it necessary to destroy those manifests already microfilmed. Within a week, Central Office provided him with copies of the 1945 disposal authority.[17]

INS sold the old New York manifests to General Waste Products, Inc., for $1,274.90 in January 1948. On January 20, the first of three railroad cars full of original manifests were made into pulp at the Crocker, Burbank and Co. Association Mill #9. The complete destruction of Ellis Island manifests on January 20, 22, and 27 was certified by the mill superintendent and an INS witness from the Boston District Office.[18]

Fifty years later, thousands of researchers around the country curse immigration manifest microfilm. The quality of the film is often poor. When the federal government began to adopt the new technology of microfilm, INS was one of the first agencies to contract for filming such a large series of records, and filming the oversized manifests was a grand experiment. Scratches on the film date from that first hot summer of 1943, and daily use by the INS exacerbated the problem. The National Archives' copies of the microfilm did not experience such heavy use until more recent decades.

Those who struggle with the microfilm may try to take comfort in this thought: Had they not been microfilmed, a copy of the immigration manifests might not be available at the National Archives. The INS's constant use of the original records would have worn them out completely if they had not been preserved in some way. Had they been laminated, as was once suggested, there would still be only one original copy. That official record would have remained with the INS, where arrival records are scheduled for retention for only one hundred years. Had they not been microfilmed, originals for the years 1892 through 1895 would already be destroyed, and those manifests of immigrants who arrived in 1896 and later would be on their way to destruction.[19]

Endnotes

1 Memorandum, Joseph Savoretti to Commissioner Earl G. Harrison, May 6, 1944, INS file 56134/715, Immigration and Naturalization Service.

2 Memorandums, Perry M. Oliver to New York District Director W. Frank Watkins, May 13, 1944; Watkins to Oliver, May 17, 1944; all in Oliver to Watkins, May 20, 1944, INS file 56134/715.

3 Memorandums, L[eonard] G. Townsend to L.A. Geyer, Sept. 29, 1944; Townsend to Oliver, Sept. 29, 1944, p. 1, INS file 56134/715.

4 Memorandum, Acting Commissioner Savoretti to Watkins, Sept. 29, 1944, INS file 56134/715.

5 Memorandum, Watkins to Savoretti, Oct. 6, 1944, INS file 56134/715.

6 George A. Cameron Jr., Graphic Microfilm Service, Inc., to Townsend, Aug. 14, 1943, p. 1, INS file 56134/715. The INS solved the dust and cinder problem in New York by installing partitions and filtering fans

during the fall of 1943. This remedy, however, only increased the temperature in the microfilm room during the summer of 1944. "[T]here have been several cases of fainting clerks," reported Mr. Townsend, "and a genuine endeavor on the part of the survivors to get out of the room as quickly and for as long a period as possible." Air-conditioning was subsequently installed. Memorandum, Townsend to Geyer, July 22, 1944, INS file 56134/715.

[7] Memorandum, Oliver to Savoretti, Oct. 12, 1944, INS file 56134/715.

[8] Memorandum, Savoretti to Watkins, Oct. 18, 1944, INS file 56134/715.

[9] Watkins to Savoretti, Oct. 21, 1944, INS file 56134/715.

[10] Savoretti to Oliver, Oct. 23, 1944, INS file 56134/715.

[11] One wonders how Reitzel felt about destroying the original manifests. He closed his memorandum by making clear the decision did "not undertake to offer any opinion on any matter except the legal question as to the admissibility in evidence of the microfilmed copies." Acting General Counsel Albert E. Reitzel to Oliver, Nov. 13, 1944, INS file 56134/715.

[12] Memorandums, Watkins to Oliver, Feb. 22, 1945; Deputy Commissioner Thomas B. Shoemaker to Oliver, Feb. 22, 1945; and "Memorandum for File" (Geyer), Mar. 17, 1945, all in INS file 56134/715B.

[13] Memorandums, Oliver to Watkins, May 8, 1945; Ralph H. Holton to Oliver, May 12, 1945; and Townsend to Geyer, May 17, 1945, all in INS file 56134/715B.

[14] Memorandum, Commissioner of Immigration and Naturalization Ugo Carusi to Watkins, May 23, 1945, and transmittal slip annotated by Mr. Carusi, May 23, 1945, INS file 56134/715B.

[15] Form G-38, Files Inventory and Appraisal (NY 000163), May 25, 1945, INS file 56241/103 ("Disposition of useless paper, New York District"), box 16, accession 85-59A2038.

[16] Memorandum, Holton to Oliver, June 5, 1945; transmittal slip (Carusi's approval), June 6, 1945; and Oliver to T. F. Higgins, June 7, 1945, INS file 56134/715B.

[17] Memorandums, New York District Administrative Officer Trent Doser to Commissioner, Dec. 18, 1947; Assistant Commissioner for Administration H. R. Landon to Watkins, Dec. 23, 1947, INS file 56214/103.

[18] Memorandums, Doser to the Commissioner, Feb. 11 and 20, 1948; Certificates of Disposal dated Jan. 20, 22, 27, and 28, 1948, INS file 56214/103.

[19] These dates apply, of course, to all ports of entry other than New York. Due to a fire in mid-June 1897, INS Ellis Island manifests only date back to June 1897.

Immigration and Passenger List Forms

CUSTOMS LIST 1821–1882

Ship Master _____

Ship Name _____

Port of Embarkation _____

Port of Arrival _____

Date of Arrival _____

Source _____

Names	Age		Sex	Occupation	The country to which they severally belong.	The country in which they intend to become inhabitants.	Died on the voyage.
	Years	Months					

CUSTOMS LIST 1883–1897

Ship Master

Ship Name

Manifest Number

Date of Embarkation

Date of Arrival

Source

List no.	Names	Age		Sex	Calling or occupation.	Native country.	Intended destination (state or country).
		Years	Months				

CUSTOMS LIST 1883–1897, continued

Ship Master

Ship Name

Manifest Number

Date of Embarkation

Date of Arrival

Source

Location of compartment or space occupied (forward, amidships or aft).	Number of pieces of baggage.	Transient, in transit or intending protracted sojourn.	Port of embarkation.	Date and cause of death.	Able to	
					Read	Write

IMMIGRATION PASSENGER LIST 1897–1903

Ship Name _____ Date of Embarkation _____ Port of Embarkation _____

Date of Arrival _____ Volume/Group _____ Source _____

| No. on list. | Name in full. | Age | | Sex | Married or single. | Calling or occupation. | Able to | | Nationality | Last residence. | Seaport of destination in U.S. |
		Years	Months				Read	Write			
1	2	3	3	4	5	6	7	7	8	9	10

IMMIGRATION PASSENGER LIST 1897–1903, continued

Ship Name

Date of Embarkation

Port of Embarkation

Date of Arrival

Volume/Group

Source

Final destination in U.S. (state, city, or town).	Whether having a ticket?	By whom was passage paid?	Having $30. If not, how much?	Even been in U.S.? If so, name and address of relative.	Going to join relative? If so, name and address of relative.	Ever in prison, almshouse, or supported by charity? Which?
11	12	13	14	15	16	17

IMMIGRATION PASSENGER LIST 1897–1903, continued

Ship Name

Date of Embarkation

Port of Embarkation

Date of Arrival

Volume/Group

Source

Supplement to immigration passenger list

Polygamist?	Contract laborer?	Condition of health? Mental and physical?	Deformed or crippled? Nature and cause?	Color	Nativity		Mother tongue (language or dialect).	Subject of what country?	Religion
					Country	Province			
18	19	20	21						

IMMIGRATION PASSENGER LIST 1903–1907

Ship Name

Date of Embarkation

Port of Embarkation

Date of Arrival

Volume/Group

Source

| No. on list. | Name in full. | Age | | Sex | Married or single. | Calling or occupation. | Able to | | Nationality (country of last permanent residence). | Race or people. | Last residence (province, city, or town). |
		Years	Months				Read	Write			
1	2	3	3	4	5	6	7	7	8	9	10

IMMIGRATION PASSENGER LIST 1903–1907, continued

Ship Name

Date of Embarkation

Port of Embarkation

Date of Arrival

Volume/Group

Source

Final destination (state, city, or town).	Whether having a ticket?	By whom was passage paid?	Whether in possession of $50. If not, how much?	Even in U.S.? If so, when and where?	Going to join relative? If so, name and address of relative.	Ever in prison, almshouse, or supported by charity? Which?
11	12	13	14	15	16	17

IMMIGRATION PASSENGER LIST 1903–1907, continued

Ship Name

Date of Embarkation

Port of Embarkation

Date of Arrival

Volume/Group

Source

Attached slip after 29 June 1906

Polygamist?	Anarchist?	Contract laborer?	Condition of health? Mental and physical?	Deformed or crippled? Nature and cause.	Personal description Height Feet	Inches	Complexion	Color of Hair	Eyes	Marks of Identification.	Place of birth.
18	19	20	21								

IMMIGRATION PASSENGER LIST 1907–1913

Ship Name

Date of Embarkation

Port of Embarkation

Date of Arrival

Volume/Group

Source

| No. on list. | Name in full. | | Age | | Sex | Married or single. | Calling or occupation. | Able to | | Nationality (country of which citizen or subject). |
	Family name.	Given name.	Years	Months				Read	Write	
1	2	2	3	3	4	5	6	7	7	8

IMMIGRATION PASSENGER LIST 1907–1913, continued

Ship Name

Date of Embarkation

Port of Embarkation

Date of Arrival

Volume/Group

Source

Race or people.	Last permanent residence.		Name and address of nearest relative or friend in country whence alien came.	Final destination.	
	Country	City or town.		State	City or town.
9	10	10	11	12	12

IMMIGRATION PASSENGER LIST 1913–1917

Ship Name

Date of Embarkation

Port of Embarkation

Date of Arrival

Volume/Group

Source

| No. on list. | Name in full. | | Age | | Sex | Married or single. | Calling or occupation. | Able to | | Nationality (country of which citizen or subject). |
	Family name.	Given name.	Years	Months				Read	Write	
1	2	2	3	3	4	5	6	7	7	8

IMMIGRATION PASSENGER LIST 1913–1917, continued

Ship Name

Date of Arrival

Date of Embarkation

Port of Embarkation

Volume/Group

Source

Race or people.	Last permanent residence.		Name and address of nearest relative or friend in country whence alien came.	Final destination.	
	Country	City or town.		State	City or town.
9	10	10	11	12	12

IMMIGRATION PASSENGER LIST 1913–1917, continued

Ship Name _____

Date of Embarkation _____

Port of Embarkation _____

Date of Arrival _____

Volume/Group _____

Source _____

No. on list.	Whether having a ticket.	By whom was passage paid?	Whether in possession of $50. If not, how much?	Ever in U.S.?			Going to join relative? If so, name and address of relative.	Ever in prison or almshouse?	Polygamist?	Anarchist?	Contract laborer?
				Yes/no	If yes—						
					Years	Where?					
13	14	15	16	17	17	17	18	19	20	21	22

IMMIGRATION PASSENGER LIST 1913–1917, continued

Ship Name

Date of Embarkation

Port of Embarkation

Date of Arrival

Volume/Group

Source

| Health condition? | Deformed or crippled? | Height | | Complexion | Color of | | Marks of identification. | Place of birth. | |
		Feet	Inches		Hair	Eyes		Country	City or town.
23	24	25	25	26	27	27	28	29	29

IMMIGRATION PASSENGER LIST 1917–1942

Ship Name

Date of Embarkation

Port of Embarkation

Date of Arrival

Volume/Group

Source

No. on list.	Head-tax status.	Name in full.		Age		Sex	Married or single.	Calling or occupation.	Able to			Nationality (country of which citizen or subject).
		Family name.	Given name.	Years	Months				Read	Language	Write	
1	2	3	3	4	4	5	6	7	8	8	8	9

IMMIGRATION PASSENGER LIST 1917–1942, continued

Ship Name

Date of Embarkation

Port of Embarkation

Date of Arrival

Volume/Group

Source

Race or people.	Last permanent residence.		Name and address of nearest relative or friend in country whence alien came.	Final destination.	
	Country	City or town.		State	City or town.
10	11	11	12	13	13

IMMIGRATION PASSENGER LIST 1917–1942, continued

Ship Name

Date of Embarkation

Port of Embarkation

Date of Arrival

Volume/Group

Source

No. on list.	Whether having a ticket.	By whom was passage paid?	Whether in possession of $50. If not, how much?	Ever in U.S.?			Going to join relative? If so, name and address of relative.	Purpose of coming to United States.			Ever in prison or almshouse?
					If yes—			Whether alien intends to return to country whence he came after engaging temporarily in laboring pursuits in the United States.	Length of time alien intends to remain in the United States.	Whether alien intends to become a citizen of the United States.	
				Yes/no	Years	Where?					
14	15	16	17	18	18	18	19	20	20	20	21

IMMIGRATION PASSENGER LIST 1917–1942, continued

Ship Name

Date of Arrival

Port of Embarkation

Date of Embarkation

Source

Volume/Group

Polygamist?	Anarchist?	Whether a person who believes in or advocates the overthrow by force or violence of the United States or all forms of law, etc.	Contract laborer?	Whether alien has been previously deported within one year.	Health condition?	Deformed or crippled?	Height Feet	Inches	Complexion	Color of Hair	Eyes	Marks of identification.	Place of birth Country	City or town.
22	23	24	25	26	27	28	29	29	30	31	31	32	33	33

Bibliography

PASSENGER LISTS, IMMIGRATION, AND NATURALIZATION

Abbott, Edith. *Immigration: Select Documents and Case Records*. Chicago: University of Chicago Press, 1924.

Allan, Morton. *Morton Allan Directory of European Passenger Steamship Arrivals for the Years 1890 to 1930 at the Port of New York and for the Years 1904 to 1926 at the Ports of New York, Philadelphia, Boston, and Baltimore*. Reprint. Baltimore: Genealogical Publishing Co., 1979.

Anuta, Michael J. *Ships of Our Ancestors*. Menominee, Mich.: Ships of Our Ancestors, Inc., 1983.

Carmack, Sharon DeBartolo. *A Genealogist's Guide to Discovering Your Immigrant and Ethnic Ancestors*. Cincinnati: Betterway Books, 2000.

Colletta, John Philip. *They Came in Ships*. Rev. ed. Orem, Utah: Ancestry Inc., 2002.

Filby, P. William. *Passenger and Immigration Lists Bibliography, 1538–1900: Being a Guide to Published Lists of Arrivals in the United States and Canada*. Detroit: Gale Research Co., 1981; supplement, 1984; 2d ed., 1988.

Guide to Genealogical Research in the National Archives. Rev. ed. Washington, D.C.: National Archives Trust Fund Board, 1985.

Hutchinson, E.P. *Legislative History of American Immigration Policy, 1798–1965*. Philadelphia: University of Pennsylvania Press, 1981.

Immigrant and Passenger Arrivals: A Select Catalog of National Archives Microfilm Publications. Washington, D.C.: National Archives Trust Fund Board, 1983. Also available online at <www.archives.gov/publications/microfilm_catalogs/immigrant/immigrant_passenger_arrivals.html>.

Jones, Maldwyn. *Destination America*. New York: Holt, Rinehart and Winston, 1976.

Kansas, Sidney. *U.S. Immigration; Exclusion and Deportation, and Citizenship of the United States of America*. 3d ed. Albany, N.Y.: Matthew Bender Co., 1948.

Kludas, Arnold. *Great Passenger Ships of the World*. 5 vols. Cambridge: Stephens, 1975–1977.

Kraut, Alan M. *Silent Travelers: Germs, Genes, and the "Immigrant Menace."* New York: Basic Books, 1994.

Newman, John J. *American Naturalization Processes and Procedures, 1790–1985*. Indianapolis: Indiana Historical Society, 1985. Reprint: Bountiful, Utah: Heritage Quest, 1998.

Schaefer, Christina K. *Guide to Naturalization Records of the United States*. Baltimore: Genealogical Publishing Co., 1997.

Smith, Eugene W. *Passenger Ships of the World, Past and Present*. Boston: George H. Dean Co., 1978.

Smith, Marian L. "The Creation and Destruction of Ellis Island Immigration Manifests." 2 parts. *Prologue* 28 (Fall 1996): 240-245; (Winter 1996): 314-318.

———. "Interpreting U.S. Immigration Manifest Annotations." *Avotaynu: The International Review of Jewish Genealogy* XII (Spring 1996): 10-13.

———. "Manifest Markings: Record of Aliens Held for Special Inquiry." <www.jewishgen.org/infofiles/manifests/bsi>.

———. "Women and Naturalization, ca. 1802–1940." *Prologue* 30 (Summer 1998): 146-153.

Smolenyak, Megan Smolenyak. *They Came to America: Finding Your Immigrant Ancestors*. San Francisco, Calif.: Santa Fe Ventures, Inc., 2002.

Szucs, Loretto Dennis. *They Became Americans: Finding Naturalization Records and Ethnic Origins*. Salt Lake City: Ancestry Inc., 1998.

Tepper, Michael H. *American Passenger Arrival Records: A Guide to the Records of Immigrants Arriving at American Ports by Sail and Steam*. Rev. ed. Baltimore: Genealogical Publishing Co., 1993.

U.S. Citizenship and Immigration Services. *An Immigrant Nation: United States Regulation of Immigration, 1798–1991*. <http://uscis.gov/graphics/aboutus/history/cover.htm>.

STEERAGE AND THE IMMIGRANT EXPERIENCE

Brandenburg, Broughton. *Imported Americans*. New York: F.A. Stokes Co., 1904.

Marshall, Edward. "Makes Six Ocean Trips to Study Steerage Reform." *New York Times*, Sunday, 30 November 1913, page SM10.

Price, Willard. "What I Learned by Traveling from Naples to New York in the Steerage." *The Italians: Social Backgrounds of an American Group*. Edited by Francesco Cordasco and Eugene Bucchioni. Clifton, N.J.: Augustus M. Kelley Publ., 1974. Originally published in *World Outlook* 3 (October 1917): 3-5, 14.

"Steerage Report Stirs Ocean Lines." *New York Times*, Wednesday, 15 December 1909, page 3, column 4.

Steiner, Edward A. *On the Trail of the Immigrant*. 5th ed. New York: Fleming H. Revell Co., 1906.

ELLIS ISLAND

Bass, Thomas A. "A New Life Begins for the Island of Hope and Tears." *Smithsonian* (June 1990).

Benton, Barbara. *Ellis Island: A Pictorial History*. New York: Facts on File, 1985.

Bolino, August C. *The Ellis Island Source Book*. Washington, D.C.: Kensington Historical Press, 1985.

Brownstone, David M., Irene M. Franck, and Douglass L. Brownstone. *Island of Hope, Island of Tears*. New York: Rawson, Wade Publishers, 1979.

Chermayeff, Ivan, Fred Wasserman, and Mary J. Shapiro. *Ellis Island: An Illustrated History of the Immigrant Experience*. New York: Macmillan Publishing Co., 1991.

Coan, Peter Morton. *Ellis Island Interviews: In Their Own Words*. New York: Facts on File, 1997.

Dunne, Thomas, and Wilton Tifft. *Ellis Island*. New York: W.W. Norton and Co., Inc., 1971.

Ellis Island Immigration Museum. "Ellis Island History: The Inspection Process." <www.ellisisland.com/inspection.html>.

Freeman, Allen. "Ellis Island Revisited." *Historic Preservation* (Sept.–Oct. 1990).

Guber, Rafael. "When Genealogists Read History, Part 2." <www.ancestry.com/library/view/ancmag/847.asp>.

Hall, Alice J. "New Life for Ellis Island." *National Geographic* (Sept. 1990): 88-101.

Holzer, Harold. "Ellis Island's Rebirth." *Americana* (Sept.–Oct. 1990).

Horn, Cathy. "The Forgotten of Ellis Island: Deaths in Quarantine, 1909–

1911." <http://freepages.genealogy.rootsweb.com/~quarantine/index.htm>.

Kinney, Doris G. "Reopening the Gateway to America." *Life* (Sept. 1990).

Moreno, Barry. *Encyclopedia of Ellis Island*. Westport, Conn.: Greenwood Press, 2004.

Oxford, Edward. "Hope, Tears, and Remembrance" and "A Treasure Rescued." *American History Illustrated* (Oct 1990).

Pitkin, Thomas M. *Keepers of the Gate: A History of Ellis Island*. New York: New York University Press, 1975.

Roberts, Jayare. "Ellis Island and the Making of America." *Genealogical Journal* 23 (1995), numbers 2 & 3: 51-142.

———. "Ellis Island Bibliography" and "Ellis Island Update." *Genealogical Journal* 23 (1995), number 4.

Seitz, Sharon, and Stuart Miller. *The Other Islands of New York City: A History and Guide*. 2d ed. Woodstock, Vt.: The Countryman Press, 2001.

Shapiro, Mary J. *Gateway to Liberty: The Story of the Statue of Liberty and Ellis Island*. New York: Vintage Books, 1986.

Szucs, Loretto Dennis. *Ellis Island: Tracing Your Family History through America's Gateway*. Rev. ed. Provo, Utah: Ancestry Publishing, 2000.

Tifft, Wilton S. *Ellis Island*. Chicago: Contemporary Books, Inc. 1990.

Yans-McLaughlin, Virginia, and Marjorie Lightman. *Ellis Island and the Peopling of America: The Official Guide*. New York: New Press, 1997.

NOVELS WITH ELLIS ISLAND AS A SETTING AND THEME

Library/Archive Source

Note: Numerous children's books have been written about Ellis Island and the immigrant experience.

Barr, Nevada. *Liberty Falling*. New York: Putnam, 1999.

Bowen, Rhys. *Murphy's Law*. New York: St. Martin's Paperbacks, 2001.

Soos, Troy. *Island of Tears*. New York: Kensington Books, 2001.

Stewart, Fred Mustard. *Ellis Island*. New York: Morrow, 1983.

VIDEO PRESENTATIONS

Island of Hope, Island of Tears. New York: Ellis Island Immigration Museum, 1992.

ADDITIONAL SOURCES

Chapter 1

Bukowczyk, John J. *And My Children Did Not Know Me: A History of the Polish-Americans.* Bloomington: Indiana University Press, 1987.

Mangione, Jerre, and Ben Morreale. *La Storia: Five Centuries of the Italian American Experience.* New York: HarperCollins, 1992.

Miller, Kerby A. *Emigrants and Exiles: Ireland and the Irish Exodus to North America.* New York: Oxford University Press, 1985.

Smith, Marian L. "American Names / Declaring Independence." <http://uscis.gov/graphics/aboutus/history/articles/nameessay.html>.

Taylor, Maureen. *Identifying Your Family Photographs.* Cincinnati: Family Tree Books, 2005.

Chapter 2

Kanellos, Nicolas, with Christelia Cristelia Pérez. *Chronology of Hispanic-American History: From Pre-Columbian Times to the Present.* New York: Gale Research, 1995.

Chapter 5

Baca, Leo, comp. *Czech Immigration Passenger Lists.* 7 vols. Richardson, Tex.: the author, 1983–1999.

Croom, Emily Anne. *The Genealogist's Companion and Sourcebook.* 2d ed. Cincinnati: Betterway Books, 2003.

Glazier, Ira A. *The Famine Immigrants: Lists of Irish Immigrants Arriving at the Port of New York, 1846–1851.* 7 vols. Baltimore: Genealogical Publishing Co., 1983–1986.

———. *Migration from the Russian Empire: Lists of Passengers Arriving at the Port of New York.* 6 vols. Baltimore: Genealogical Publishing Co., 1995–1997.

Glazier, Ira A., and P. William Filby. *Germans to America: Lists of Passengers Arriving at U.S. Ports.* 67+ volumes. Wilmington, Del.: Scholarly Resources, 1988–2002.

———. *Italians to America: Lists of Passengers Arriving at U.S. Ports, 1880–1899.* 16 vols. Wilmington, Del.: Scholarly Resources, 1992–2002.

Index to Emigrants from Sweden to New York, 1851–1869. Salt Lake City: Genealogical Society of Utah, 1987–1988.

Lainhart, Ann S. *State Census Records*. Baltimore: Genealogical Publishing Co., 2000.

Olsen, Nils William, and Erik Wikén. *Swedish Passenger Arrivals in the United States, 1820–1850*. Stockholm: Schmidts Boktryckeri AB, 1995.

Potter, Constance. "St. Albans Passenger Arrival Records." *Prologue* 22 (Spring 1990): 90-93.

Swierenga, Robert P. *Dutch Immigrants in U.S. Ship Passenger Manifests, 1820–1880: An Alphabetical Listing by Household Heads and Independent Persons*. 2 vols. Wilmington, Del.: Scholarly Resources, 1983.

Voultsos, Mary, comp. *Greek Immigrant Passengers, 1885–1910*. 4 vols. Worcester, Mass.: the author, 1991.

Chapter 7

Bodnar, John. *The Transplanted: A History of Immigrants in Urban America*. Bloomington: Indiana University Press, 1985.

"Caring for Immigrants." *New York Times*, 16 June 1897, page 1.

Cerase, Francesco. "Expectations and Reality: A Case Study of Return Migration from the United States to Southern Italy." *International Migration Review* 8 (1974): 246-262.

Daniels, Roger. *Coming to America: A History of Immigration and Ethnicity in American Life*. 2d ed. New York: Perennial, 2002.

DeConde, Alexander. *Half Bitter, Half Sweet: An Excursion into Italian-American History*. New York: Charles Scribner's Sons, 1971.

"Fire on Ellis Island." *New York Times*, 15 June 1897, page 1.

Giordano, Joseph, ed. *The Italian American Catalog*. Garden City, N.Y.: Doubleday, 1986.

"Immigrants on the Piers." *New York Times*, 17 June 1897, page 12.

Sowell, Thomas. *Ethnic America: A History*. New York: Basic Books, 1981.

Speranza, Gino C. "How It Feels to Be a Problem." *Charities* XII, no. 18 (May 1904): 457-463.

Chapter 10

Carmack, Sharon DeBartolo. *You Can Write Your Family History*. Cincinnati: Betterway Books, 2003.

Taylor, Maureen A. *Scrapbooking Your Family History*. Cincinnati: Betterway Books, 2003.

Index